D0422459

The Dictionary of Disruption

Also available from Continuum

Managing Very Challenging Behaviour, Louisa Leaman

Naked Teacher, Louisa Leaman

Classroom Confidential, Louisa Leaman

Dos and Don'ts of Behaviour Management 2nd Edition, Roger Dunn

Managing Boys' Behaviour, Tabatha Rayment

Managing Behaviour in the Early Years, Janet Kay

Getting the Buggers to Behave 3rd Edition, Sue Cowley

Managing Your Classroom 2nd Edition, Gererd Dixie

The Dictionary of Disruption

A Practical Guide to Behaviour Management

Louisa Leaman

continuum

Continuum International Publishing Group

The Tower Building   80 Maiden Lane, Suite 704

11 York Road   New York, NY 10038

SE1 7NX

www.continuumbooks.com

© Louisa Leaman 2007

British Library Cataloguing-in-Publication Data
A catalogue record for this book is available from the British Library.

ISBN: 0-8264-9047-6 (paperback)

Library of Congress Cataloging-in-Publication Data
A catalog record for this book is available from the Library of Congress.

Typeset by ISB Typesetting, Sheffield
Printed and bound in Great Britain by Ashford Colour Press, Gosport, Hampshire

Contents

Introduction

The idea behind this book was prompted by the hectic, busy lifestyles that many school staff have. As a practising classroom teacher, I know only too well how manic things can get: planning, resources, assessments, targets, marking, displays, record keeping … Just as I think I've got on top of one list of tasks, another list comes along. Sometimes there seems to be so much to do, it is hard to know where to begin. And when having to manage students with difficult behaviour on top of all of this, the pressure is cranked up even more. Not only does difficult behaviour cause added stress, it also requires attention and time – and both of these things are like gold dust.

Because of these factors, I wanted to write something that gives effective, practical advice on behaviour management, in an accessible and easy-to-navigate way. The dictionary-style makes this possible. If you haven't got time to sit and wade through an entire book, just to find one useful paragraph or suggestion, *The Dictionary of Disruption* is something that can offer solutions quickly and concisely. Just turn to the section you need: if you are anticipating a terrible lesson with 7GL on Monday morning, the section on 'Group behaviour' may reassure you and give you some ideas. If you are finding it hard to get your lessons started, go to the section on 'Beginnings'. Put the book somewhere handy, as you would with a normal dictionary, and then you can get at ideas as you need them.

Hopefully you'll find that *The Dictionary of Disruption* is thoroughly comprehensive. I have endeavoured to include information on a broad range of issues, from the general to the specific, from low-level disruption through to physical assault. I have focused on *how* to do things, as well as outlining *what* to do. I have also consulted with a large number of teachers and school professionals in order to make sure that the material is relevant and realistic.

It is important to recognize how things are connected, therefore I have included links between useful or related sections. For example, if you look up 'Consequences', you will also be referred to sections on 'Rewards' and 'Detentions'. Effective behaviour management strategies do not exist in isolation from one another. They are connected and they back each other up. *The Dictionary of Disruption* will hopefully show why and how, helping teachers to practise behaviour management with integrity and clear understanding.

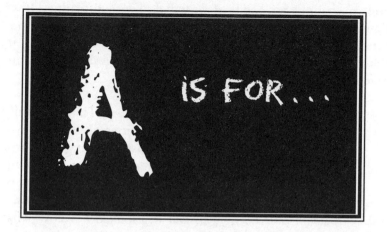

ACTING

It seems fitting that the first entry into this book should be the word 'acting', since I have heard so many teachers describe their practice in the classroom as performance. They explain, they inspire and they entertain, all in front of a willing audience of dedicated students ... in the ideal world perhaps, but maybe most classrooms are closer in nature to PT Barnum than the Royal Shakespeare Company. No one could deny the energy and enthusiasm of a circus audience. It's just that they tend to get over-excited, like to make noise and will throw things if they get bored!

The idea of 'acting' in the classroom is particularly important when considering behaviour management. The environment we create during a lesson can seem quite artificial. Do we truly care whether people are wearing baseball caps indoors or chewing gum? Perhaps not, but we may need to take issue with these things within the school walls, in order to establish that all-important sense of boundary and expectation.

An actor needs to maintain their performance if it is to be convincing. If they slip in and out of character, the illusion collapses. For us, as teachers, this means keeping up the façade, every day, every lesson. This can be very tiring. One way to make it easier is to have a clear understanding of what our boundaries and expectations are, and how we will deal with difficulties. If we figure these things out and have them firmly embedded in our thoughts, we will not forever have to be improvising (which, in the acting world, is a challenging and specialized skill). There are several effective ways in which we can do this:

1. *Establish a 'menu' of rewards and sanctions.* Think carefully about what these could be (see sections on 'Reward systems' and 'Consequences' for ideas), ensuring that there is enough range to reflect different levels of behaviour. Write them out and, if you prefer, stick them somewhere in your classroom as a reminder to you and your students.

2. *Establish class rules, rights and responsibilities.* Know what you want, and share this with your students. Class rules should be simple, positive and meaningful (see section on 'Rules' for more information). Write them up and place them where they are visible, which will help to keep them in your consciousness.

3. *Have a set of classroom routines.* Structure and routine allows people to feel more secure and confident in their surroundings. During transition times (lesson beginnings, ends and changes of activity), the use of routines – or lack of – will affect student behaviour, and may ultimately affect the stability of the rest of the lesson. Decide on some simple, enforceable routines and then stick to them (see section on 'Routines' for suggestions).

4. *Learn your lines.* Being creative with words is all part of the fun of being a teacher, but when dealing with difficult behaviour, straightforward and repetitive language is usually the most effective. Knowing a few key phrases (see section on 'Useful phrases') can help you to feel prepared and enable you to perform under pressure.

5. *Rehearse!* Take a few moments before each day/lesson begins to focus on what you want to achieve, and to anticipate some of the hurdles and how you might deal with them. A bit of mental preparation will make the curtain-lifting moment less daunting.

ANGER

Anger and angry behaviour can be hazardous in the classroom, as it can lead to aggressive activity, and is unsettling for everyone. Fortunately, more extreme angry outbursts are not frequent occurrences in mainstream schools and lower-level outbursts can be dealt with very effectively, if approached in the right way. First of all it is important to be able to recognize the early warning signs of an angry individual:

- Physical agitation (e.g., pacing up and down, twitching, clenched fists, fiddling with equipment)
- Changes in facial expression (clenched teeth, furrowed brow, frowning, looking flushed, staring or averting gaze)
- Changes in posture (tense muscles, hunched shoulders, arms folded)
- Verbal challenges ('Make me … go on then!')
- Over sensitivity to suggestions or comments.

If a student is presenting angry behaviours, your main concern should be to diffuse their distress. Approach them in a passive way, using a quiet voice and empathy ('I can see that you are upset …'), and avoid reacting in an aggressive, impatient manner, which will only exacerbate the problem. Do not expect immediate results, because angry people can get 'locked into' their emotions. Don't drone on about what they should/should not be doing – diffusing the anger is your primary concern. If necessary, offer them some time and/or space to themselves (for a more thorough look at calming down a crisis, see section on 'De-escalation'). Here are some examples (based on real experiences). A good one …

Tina has entered the room in a bad mood. When you ask her to remove her coat (like everyone else), she refuses and becomes agitated and angry.
TEACHER: Tina, I'd like you to remove your coat, along with everyone else please.
TINA: Tch … NO.
TEACHER: Tina?
TINA: I'm not taking it off. You can't make me!

Tina frowns and clenches her fists. The teacher walks calmly towards her, and stands beside her. Tina tries to turn away, but the teacher crouches down to her level and initiates eye-contact.

TEACHER: Tina? I can see that something is really bothering you ... I wonder if I can help?

TINA: *Tch* ... go away! Leave me alone!

TEACHER: Well, you know I can't do that ... because this is my classroom ... but I want to make sure that you're feeling okay. Why don't you take a few minutes and go and sit at the back of the room, where you can have some peace and quiet to calm down. I'll get the lesson started, and then I'll come and have a chat with you ...

Tina agrees and goes to the back of the room. Five minutes later, she removes her coat and voluntarily joins the rest of the class. The teacher looks over, and Tina gives her a nod, as if to say 'I'm better now, thanks.'

And a bad one ...

Same situation, different teacher.

TEACHER: Tina, take your coat off now!

TINA: *Tch* ... NO!

TEACHER: Uh ... I don't have time for this! Take it off now, please!

TINA: MAKE ME ... GO ON THEN!

The teacher sighs and then shouts across the room at her.

TEACHER: STOP WASTING EVERYONE'S TIME AND TAKE YOUR COAT OFF – YOU KNOW YOU'RE NOT SUPPOSED TO WEAR IT IN CLASS.

Tina slams her chair back and stands up.

TINA: STOP SHOUTING AT ME!

TEACHER: SIT DOWN!

Tina picks up her bag and storms out of the room. After she has left, her well-meaning classmates inform the teacher that he's 'well out of order' for having a go at her, because recently she's been upset about her mum and dad splitting up.

Anger is an acceptable feeling to have: it is an instinctive reaction to the things we experience and the way we feel about them. We can be angry, but we need to know how to do this without causing hurt to ourselves, or others. As teachers, we can reinforce this message by creating opportunities for students to talk about their feelings, and by modelling non-angry behaviours. Although unfortunately, there are many messages to the contrary: film, TV and sporting personalities often legitimize angry behaviour, parents tell their children to 'fight back', and peer groups often revere 'toughness'.

APOLOGIES

Not everyone may agree, but I have always considered the apology to be an important part of the behaviour management process. Of course 'sorry' is only a word, and is often given too emptily and accepted too freely, but if used with care, it becomes a powerful emblem for ownership, responsibility and forgiveness. I have gone to great lengths in order to elicit meaningful apologies from students, and it has always been worth it. I have also refused to acknowledge apologies that are less than sincere, because unless the student is looking inward and genuinely taking ownership of their actions, accepting an apology can be counter-productive – think of the student who puts on an Oscar-winning display of regret, then winks at his mates as he walks back through the door! So how do you get a sincere apology quickly and efficiently, without wasting precious teaching time?

1. *Do it when ready.* No one finds saying sorry easy, and it can be even harder in the heat of the moment. You may want to allow time to pass before you pursue it, giving the student(s) a chance to calm down and, hopefully, reflect, but also allowing you to carry on with your lesson. 'I will speak to you at the end of the lesson' or, if appropriate, 'I'd like you to wait outside, and I'll come and speak to you in a few minutes' will both prepare them and allow them space.

2. *Be discreet.* Wherever possible, obtain apologies in privacy – either by stepping outside the classroom door, waiting until after the lesson or addressing the individual quietly within the class. It is unlikely that you will get a favourable response if the student in question is being ogled by his/ her peers.

3. *Be firm.* Address the student calmly, but as though you mean business. Look out for their mannerisms. Do they

look ready to take it seriously? Are they calm enough? Do they need to be reminded to look at you, to stop slouching on the radiator, to stop smirking? Restate the reason why they are expected to apologize, or preferably, ask them to do it (encouraging them to reflect on their actions). A barely audible mutter is not enough. I favour the 'sorry … *why are you sorry?* … I'm sorry because … *thank you and what will you do to put it right?*' approach.

4. *'Show' not tell.* When a student's difficult behaviour has been repetitive, it may be time for the 'show-not-tell' explanation: 'You've said sorry a lot of times, but then you've carried on with the behaviour. The word has lost its meaning now. This time you need to *show* me you mean it, by making an effort not to do it any more.'

5. *Accept sincere apologies.* If an apology is a way of acting responsibly, then it needs to be met with equivalent graciousness. End the conversation on a positive note: 'Thank you. I accept your apology, and I look forward to seeing you settle back into class in a positive way.'

6. *Give sincere apologies.* Lead by example. If you have made a mistake or a misjudgement, you are more likely to earn back your respect points, by showing that you are able to admit to this, than by trying to play the 'teacher is always right' card.

ASPIRATION

How many times have you questioned your efforts to support and encourage certain students, because they themselves never seem to care whether they achieve in school or not? Aspiration – the motivation to make progress – is one of the keystones of academic performance. Today's students are constantly told that education will define their opportunities for the future. Employers want people that are literate and articulate. Colleges want to see at least 5 A★–Cs. Close the door now, and it will be harder to open later. The carrot of future success (the fast cars, big money and flash clothes) is dangled alluringly, in the hope that it will entice them to knuckle down and focus.

The reality is that many young people lack or are confused about their aspirations and future ambitions, or may simply be too interested in what is going on now (the latest episode of *Big Brother*/Kayleigh's new boyfriend/how many ring-tones has your phone got), to care about what will happen to them in five years' time. Unfortunately, this can translate into underachievement and, often, poor behaviour.

Getting through to a student whose behaviour in school is underlined by a chronic lack of aspiration can feel very fruitless. So they haven't handed in homework again? *So?* So they've bunked off three lessons, and missed a piece of coursework? *So?* So they're in detention, for a week? *Bovvered?* Not really. This is the most challenging part of the behaviour management process. No matter how experienced or inspirational a teacher you are, if you are contending with the aspiration problem, you are fighting a tough battle.

I do not believe in lost causes, but I feel it is important to recognize that many of the underlying reasons why an individual might misbehave and disengage with their education are far more complex than schools, alone, can deal with. Aspiration begins in the home (how many of your unmotivated students have unmotivated parents?). It is also influenced by the many and varied messages that people are bombarded with: from their peers, from their role models, from the media. As teachers, we can promote a positive learning environment and emphasize that our actions have consequences, but we cannot single-handedly unravel the perils of society at large.

I have one simple piece of advice: get to know your students. *Especially* the difficult ones. Surprise them by taking an interest – a light-hearted chat in the corridor, or a bit of 'banter' after class. Establish a connection, and then use this to nurture a positive relationship. The next time they misbehave, remind them that even if they don't care about their education and future, *you* do. The fact that they may now have a trace of respect for you means they might just value your opinion.

ASSERTIVENESS

During my teacher training, it was noted that I had a 'big' voice. I was encouraged to use this to my advantage, by developing an assertive tone and using it to get my point across, in place of shouting or snapping. This advice has served me well, and I now believe that assertiveness is one of the most important skills a teacher can develop. We are in the business of making people cooperate, listen and follow codes of behaviour – sometimes against their will. If we cannot do this convincingly and rationally, we will get ourselves into bother.

Being assertive is about being self-assured, about projecting an air of confidence. It is also about expectations. If we know what we want from our students, and are clear about our classroom boundaries, then finding the right words and reactions will come more readily. It is not about shouting or being unduly aggressive – we should never think we can 'make' a child do anything (which only leads to frustration). We need to think of it as a means of directing our students towards better choices.

Of course, some people find that an assertive, confident manner comes naturally, whereas others may feel it has eluded them. Classrooms can be a painful place to be if you lack confidence in yourself, and there is a strong link between self-esteem and stress. Reassuringly, I'm sure that all teachers can recount times when they have felt uncertain of their craft, and I also believe that anyone can learn to express themselves more assertively. It may be necessary to do a bit of soul-searching, as assertiveness is as much about the mind, as it is body language and voice (for ideas on how to use your body and voice assertively, see sections on 'Non-verbal' and 'Verbal communication'). For guidance regarding self-esteem and emotional issues, the Teacher Support Network (TSN) may be able to help, or why not consider assertiveness training.

ATTENTION-SEEKING

So much problematic classroom behaviour seems to stem from attention-seeking, whether it is the attention of adults that is desired, or the attention of other students. It is important to understand its origins. In the most extreme cases, I find that the phrase 'attention-*need*ing' is more appropriate, because attention is inextricably linked with feelings of self-worth. Many children – and adults – are caught up in the chase to be noticed. Receiving attention from others is a way of experiencing feelings of security and validity. It is, of course, a chase in vain, because the only real way to feel secure and valid is to feel it from within: to have a healthy sense of personal self-worth.

In this context, attention-needing behaviour can be a very difficult nut to crack. Our options are to ignore it or indulge it. Ignoring can be ineffective. I have often seen students take inappropriate behaviour to more dramatic levels, if it is not addressed, because the need for attention overrides any potential consequence. Some students will develop the instinct that *any* attention is better than none, and will therefore seek out negative attention (telling off/criticism/complaint). For example:

Kyle is messing about with a ruler, flicking it across the table and creating a distracting noise whilst the teacher is talking to the class. When the teacher ignores this, he starts to bang his fists on the table. The teacher continues to ignore this behaviour, and makes a point of praising the rest of the class for listening. Eventually, Kyle starts shoving his table backwards and forwards, in a way that disrupts the students around him, forcing the teacher to focus his attention on him.

Indulging attention-needing behaviour can be time-consuming and exhausting. If it is not the all-consuming 'look-at-me NOW' type, it can be insidious and quietly irritating. Think of the student who repeatedly asks for help, frequently calls out, follows you around the room/playground, always has one problem or another … that permanent hunger for you to notice them, whilst 29 other students are trying to get noticed as well. If we suppose that the fair 'cure' for individuals who need lots of attention is to give it to them, we can quickly appreciate how unrealistic this is.

My main piece of advice for dealing with this issue is to reinforce *appropriate* ways of gaining *positive* attention, and to avoid giving *negative* attention. Do this by:

1. Ensuring that you reassure students by frequently noticing and praising examples of desired behaviour.

2. *Tactically* ignoring negative behaviour, i.e., let the student know that you are aware of it, but that you are not interested in it. Be blasé: 'I realize there is someone making silly noises over there, but it doesn't interest me ... '

3. Reinforcing this with a when/then command, using positive attention as the carrot: 'When you settle down and show me that you are getting on quietly, then I'll come and see how you are doing.'

4. Modelling or explaining appropriate ways in which a student can get attention, and then praising them when they get it right (e.g., putting their hand up, instead of calling out).

5. Encouraging students to be more independent. Try a 'Do You Need Help?' poster, with suggestions on what to do: Check again – can you work it out for yourself? Can you look it up in a book or on the Internet? Can you ask a friend?

6. Supporting students who share a class with an attention-needy individual, advising them on how to cope with unwanted provocations and showing off (move away/ask them to stop/speak to an adult), but also on how to include that individual.

7. Empathizing – can you imagine what it is like to feel as though you are always overlooked?

ATTITUDE

The most important thing to remember when dealing with students who present confrontational, cocky attitude is that it is *just a veneer*. The boy who growls and sneers and informs you that 'you can't tell him what to do ... you're not a proper teacher', when all you've done is ask him to take out his planner, is not convinced of his elevated status – he is chancing his luck. However, dealing with a group of lippy teenagers who 'can't be bovvered' with anything (unless it smells of rebellion) can be unnerving. They may be taller than you, they may dress differently and they most certainly will be prone to answering back; but dig away the layers of bravado and you will probably find a few sheep in wolf's clothing. Combat the power of negative attitude by showing you are unafraid, can see through it and are willing to listen:

1. *Promote respect.* Create opportunities for classroom discussion about respectful ways of communicating, which provides a 'safe' context in which students can air their views. Model desired behaviour.

2. *Allow students to express their opinions.* Instead of shutting down a student's cocky comments ('don't speak to me like that!'), try active listening: 'so what you are telling me is … ' Encourage them to reflect on *why* they think everything's rubbish/writing sucks/they can do what they like in school.

3. *Remain neutral.* Do not rise to remarks that are intended to hurt or undermine you. You do not want to get sucked into power struggles, or reinforce the idea that this is a way of getting one over on you. Keep calm (for help see section on 'Coping'), and show your disapproval without getting emotional: 'That comment is inappropriate/unnecessary … when you are ready to talk in a respectful way with me, then I will be happy to listen.'

AWARENESS

Knowing what is going on amongst our students, within our classrooms, is vitally important if we are to keep on top of behaviour. If we can spot the early signs of an emerging problem, and then intervene in a low-level way, we may be able to prevent the situation escalating into a big disruption. The key is in knowing our students and the things that may trigger certain behaviours, and in being *aware* of our classroom space.

My experiences of teaching in special schools for pupils with Emotional, Social and Behavioural Difficulties in small classes (of no more than ten pupils) taught me the value of being 'on the ball'. My colleagues and I used the metaphor of putting out sparks (before they start fires) to describe our practice, because so much of our efforts involved dampening down the little flare-ups that frequently occurred amongst such a volatile group of young people. To do this, we had to be incredibly alert and quick thinking – no fuzzy hangovers, or can't-quite-be-bothered-today attitudes. If we didn't 'manage' behaviour at its lowest level, things could quickly escalate out of control.

This was one of the single most exhausting aspects of the work, and made a large contribution to everyone's stress levels. When I came to work in mainstream schools, I discovered that, although the flare-ups were less regular, the sheer amount of students to keep track of made it no less stressful. Unfortunately, there is no magic cure for the pressures of being vigilant in the classroom (apart from exceptionally well-behaved children), but I do have some suggestions that may make the process easier:

1. *Work the room.* Make the most of your physical presence by moving to different areas of the classroom space as you teach, therefore giving all students the sense that you could be standing next to them at any time.

2. *Don't turn your back.* When writing on a board, turn sideways *away* from the hand that is writing, so that you can easily face out towards the room. Try strategically placing a mirror, to give you an overview of your students.

3. *Organize the space.* Are there ways in which you can rearrange your classroom furniture to aid visibility? Remember, if you keep your room tidy, it will be easier to scan for trouble.

4. *Anticipate in advance.* Anticipation will help you to know where to look and can prepare you for what might happen, enabling you to make adjustments accordingly. For instance, if certain students clash, arrange the seating so that they are separated.

5. *Know your students.* If you know their triggers, and the signs that they may be getting wound up (facial expressions, changes in voice, etc.), you will have a clearer idea of when to act.

6. *Take rest.* Make sure you get proper breaks when you can, away from the classroom and the students, where you can relax, rest and reduce the accumulative effects of the stress of concentration.

BEGINNINGS

One of the most important times in any lesson is the beginning, as it sets the tone for the rest of the session, and helps to establish an atmosphere of calm. The beginning is especially important when teaching students who have behavioural difficulties. Unstructured times and moments of transition (from one lesson to another, or between activities) have always been flash points for these individuals, and therefore need to be managed carefully.

If a lesson beginning resembles a shamboblic social gathering, in which students drift in and out, chat amongst themselves, and generally act as though they have all the time in the world, the teacher needs to tighten up. Beginnings need to be teacher-defined if they are to set a helpful tone. Too many otherwise-competent teachers fall into the trap of thinking they have an 'impossible' class, because after a few scrappy lesson beginnings they give up on high expectations and assume the students will do what they like despite their interventions. Rule number one: YOU ARE THE BOSS.

Their behaviour may be unpalatable but it won't change unless you change. You are reasonable, fair and calm, but you are the boss nonetheless, therefore *you* decide the manner and time in which your students enter the room and prepare for learning. I appreciate that this is not always easy, as it takes effort and time to establish a structured, teacher-defined start, but it can be considerably more frustrating (and time-consuming) to try clawing back a group of students who were lost the moment they stepped through the door. Some no-nonsense ideas:

1. *Be on time.* Although there may be times when lateness is unavoidable, if you expect punctuality from your students, then you should endeavour to deliver it yourself. There is nothing like standing around for 15 minutes without adult supervision to unsettle a class (I once knew a teacher who was frequently 20 minutes late to her lessons, some of which were taught in port-a-cabins, allowing students ample opportunity to sneak behind them and have a few crafty cigarettes before she arrived – not the best way to start!).

2. *Greet students personally.* If possible, stand at the door and welcome them in. This gives you the opportunity to create an inviting atmosphere, to monitor the mood of the class as they come in and to have a quick, quiet word with a few 'key' individuals (i.e., positive pep talk: 'Gary, I'm pleased to see you're on time today. We're doing algebra, and I know it's not your favourite, but I've got some fun activities planned so I think you'll do well ...')

3. *Try using a line.* If pupils are standing in an orderly fashion *before* they enter the room, the chances of them being calm once inside will increase. Troublemakers or noisy students can be told to stand on the opposite side and wait until the others have gone in (though be wary of students using this as a means to avoid entering the room). Younger students may benefit from a lining-up rules and/or points chart to remind them at the door.

4. *Use simple routines.* These should be purposeful and straight-forward, governing what you expect students to do as they enter the room: taking their seats and staying there, removing their coats, taking out their planners and lesson equipment, etc. Think about these routines carefully, as they need to be easy to enforce and solve more problems than they create. For example, is it really necessary for students to enter the room in complete silence?

5. *Take-up time.* Don't put extra pressure on yourself by believing that your students should be ready to start *immediately*. Allow a reasonable amount of time (no more than five minutes) from when they come in to when the lesson actually starts, for them (and you) to get settled. You may want to allow additional time, if the lesson falls at one of those tricky points during the day (e.g., straight after break or lunch).

6. *Clear time limit with reward.* Make this time limit explicit, so that students are aware of your expectations. A countdown can be helpful, as can the offer of incentives – an individual reward for students that are ready on time (e.g., a smiley-face stamp, point or merit mark quickly given out whilst the rest are getting ready), or a whole class reward, encouraging everyone to pull together.

7. *Starter activities.* Provide something that students can focus their attention on as soon as they enter and settle. This could be a short activity connected with the lesson, or even something simple, such as an anagram or dingbat written up on the board (if you want ideas, they often have them in the puzzle pages of the magazines that lie around the staff room). Offering a reward to the first person to get the answer right can be very motivating.

8. *With very difficult groups, enforce a seating plan.* If, despite your efforts, students are failing to cooperate at the beginning of your lessons, invest some time in taking charge of the seating arrangements. Have them wait in a line outside the door, and allow them in one by one or in small groups, allocating them pre-determined seats as you go (see section on Seating plans). They may not like it, and it may take time to organize, but it will give them a swift reminder that *you* are the boss.

9. *Try and try again.* Again, this is about investing some time to establish your position of authority in the classroom. If students enter the room in a less than satisfactory manner, send them out and make them do it again. And then again. And again. Until they are perfect. Slam your expectations into their memories. Yes, it will take up an entire lesson, but whenever I have used this strategy, I have found it to have a powerful, long-lasting effect.

10.   *Have a strategy for latecomers.* If they enter during the register or after you have started teaching, have them wait by the door or outside, so that they do not distract other students by sauntering through the rows of desks. Unless they have a note or legitimate reason, hear the excuses in *their* time, not yours (i.e., when it is convenient for you and not whilst you are in the middle of addressing the rest of the class), and have a clear sanction for persistent lateness.

11.   *Reward appropriate behaviour.* Lots of positive words and encouragement for those who come in, sit down and wait sensibly for the lesson to begin.

BEHAVIOUR

What exactly do we mean by behaviour? The English Dictionary describes the verb *behave* as to 'act or function in a particular way'. For the purposes of this book we are considering all that acting and functioning that is deemed inappropriate for the classroom. So what constitutes the inappropriate? Ultimately, this is a matter of opinion. One teacher may expect absolute silence during their lessons, another may prefer students to chat and share ideas. Some teachers may be lenient on students who do not have the right equipment, but others may be zero-tolerant.

Whatever our own personal gripes and foibles are, it is important to remember that effective schools have some kind of common ground: a leveller of behaviour expectations that all teachers aim to maintain (see section on 'Consistency'), and that are upheld by senior management and the behaviour policy, strengthening the message about what is and is not acceptable. But it is not enough to assume that, just because the expectations of behaviour make perfect sense to us ('thou shall not beat thy neighbour up in the corridor, or spoil thy learning experience for others'), they will automatically connect with the mindsets of our students – hence problem behaviour.

In my experiences, I have seen students arriving at the world of school with *no idea* of what is acceptable conduct within the classroom, which leads me to believe that their parents have ignored the widely accepted social message that swearing/ hitting/

spitting/stealing and kicking is wrong. More worryingly, there seems to be a rather large number of secondary-age students who still haven't cottoned on. So what is this all about?

Much of our personal behaviour is the result of what we have learned, through what we see others do, or how they react to us. The child that throws a tantrum because he wants sweets for his dinner, rather than a balanced nutritious meal, may decide that the behaviour works for him, if given into. Next time he realizes he is being denied his own way, out comes the kicking and screaming. Children need clear boundaries. There is no disputing that.

Many teachers have to struggle with the fact that the boundaries needed to make a classroom safe and successful are not always maintained beyond the school gates. Little Sammy is asked not to swear in the playground, but his dad has already told him he shouldn't listen to what those ****ing teachers say. This dichotomy can be hard for both students and staff to adjust to. If you are a teacher in this situation, work on the parents as much as possible (and I realize that, in some cases, this is easier said than done). The key is teamwork. If you can get them on your side, and encourage them to lay down some boundaries, then the child will have a chance of understanding what is expected of them. (See section on 'Parents' for ideas.)

The other important thing to understand about behaviour is that it can have meaning – it is a form of *communication*. Whenever I'm dealing with a problem, I always try to interpret what might be going on beneath the surface, because I believe that having an *understanding* of why something is happening is the key to resolving it. Sometimes the meaning of a student's behaviour is obvious to me, and to them: they are shouting because they are angry because another child took their things. But sometimes I can see things that the student can't, because they are so consumed by the moment: they are refusing to cooperate because they have been backed into a corner and don't want to lose face because they are worried about what other people think of them. And sometimes it is hard for both sides to tell, but even the most mindless, arbitrary-seeming actions can be trying to express something: I'm bored. I don't feel in control. I don't understand myself.

The real problem is not always the behaviour. The behaviour is a reaction to primary thoughts, feelings and triggers. Our challenge is to enable students to develop self-awareness of these thoughts, feelings and triggers, helping them to be more aware of what their primary problems are and extending their emotional confidence and vocabulary, to enable them to express their difficulties more reasonably. Easy, eh?

BONDING

Having worked in schools for young people with Emotional, Social and Behavioural Difficulties, I never underestimate the importance of getting students to 'bond'. Sometimes, this has to come before the learning experience can begin. If students are preoccupied with arguing, fighting and aggravating one another, they are not going to be in a learning frame of mind. Of course, pushing on with a lesson (particularly if it is interesting) can eventually be enough to distract them from their issues with one another, but in extreme cases, this can be an incredible struggle.

In such circumstances, and particularly in primary schools, where the timetable is more flexible, it can be helpful to spend some time focusing on activities that encourage teamwork and co-operation, but have a lot of 'appeal' (i.e., they are fun). With adult supervision, these can be a great opportunity to work on communication and cooperative skills, paving the way for smoother, calmer future lessons. Many primary school teachers will be well-versed in 'circle time', which is a great way of modelling listening, turn-taking and sharing. There are plenty of books and resources available on the subject. Less conventional activities could include:

- Orienteering challenges (in teams), either within class, around school or outdoors
- Making 'things' out of scrap materials (e.g., bridges, chairs, catapults) in teams, with a bit of gentle competition to see who comes up with the most effective design
- Small-group role-plays, exploring a familiar dilemma (e.g., what would you do if … ?), then sharing and discussing each other's decisions
- Projects (e.g., running a food stall at the school open day, planning an end-of-term party, organizing a lunchtime

sports tournament) in which students need to pull together and cooperate in order to make the event happen.

BOREDOM

Boredom is the scourge of all classrooms. If our students are bored they will quickly disengage from the learning opportunities we have so meticulously prepared for them, and more than likely, find less productive ways to amuse themselves. The task is upon us then, to find ways of making knowledge exciting and accessible (see sections on 'Kinaesthetic learning', 'Learning styles' and 'Pace' for suggestions), although we would have to be superhuman to achieve this every single lesson. The key is to establish a balance between the high-octane, creative teaching methods that hook them in, and then the steadier, gentler ones that get things done. I think it is only fair that if our students expect us to do what we can to make our lessons 'fun', that they are prepared to give something back, in other words, to graft when required. Sadly, this notion seems to have evaded a few of them …

There is always that percentage of individuals who complain of boredom as a matter of course. We could convert our classrooms into palaces of wonder, and they'd still sit there with their chins on their desks, telling us ''srubbish'. My response to them is to talk about the travelling experiences I've had, visiting developing countries where young people have immense pride and belief in education, but are often held back by poverty.

The important issue to look out for is whether the phrase, 'this is boring', is a disguised way of saying 'this is too difficult'. A student who is insecure or anxious about their academic ability may try to mask their perceived failings by avoiding the work and blaming our choice of task. The way to get round this is to look at ways in which we can make the work more obviously achievable (see section on 'Differentiation'), and, in the long term, to develop their academic self-esteem. Boredom is also a sign work is not challenging enough.

I frequently hear teachers bemoaning the National Curriculum, which limits the choice of subject content, and, coupled with the Government's penchant for performance targets, creates pressure and frustration. With challenging students, it can be even more stressful. Therefore, we need to be thoughtful about how we select and adapt the curriculum, making sure that we are covering the basics whilst making it entertaining. Some ideas:

1. *Be animated.* Talk up your love for your subject (if there is any left!), and start the lesson by telling a fun story or anecdote.
2. *Use visual material.* Laminated photographs and/or objects of reference have much more impact than pages of text. With the advent of the Internet and search engines, resources and images are easy to find.
3. *Contemporary context.* Relate events and facts to the real lives of your students, encouraging them to compare their experiences, using discussion and role-play – which can also be recorded with a camera.
4. *Competition.* Set a few simple questions at the start of your lesson, encouraging students to look out for the answers as the lesson progresses with a prize for those who get them right at the end.
5. *Make it physical.* Where possible, incorporate activities that involve students actively participating, e.g., stepping out to the front to demonstrate an action.
6. *Avoid long periods of teacher talk.* (Especially at the start of the lesson.)

BOUNDARIES

We all know we should set boundaries, but how and why? Boundaries are the divide between what is and is not acceptable. They do not just exist. They have to be established and developed through common understanding between those setting them and those following them. They are important in the classroom because they allow us to place limits on the behaviour we tolerate, making it easier to maintain a safe, calm and productive learning environment.

Many boundaries in life are implicit, governed by moral and social codes of conduct, and are supported by various mechanisms.

We know that if we commit a crime, we will face arrest and possibly prison. We also know that if we don't bother turning up to work for a few days, we may face a disciplinary and, ultimately, the sack. In the classroom, it's not so different, except that we, as teachers, need to be the ones setting up and managing these boundaries. In a sense, we get to play sheriff.

From a student's perspective, it is important that the boundaries within the classroom make sense and have a clear purpose. *Why* should we stay seated at our desks unless we have permission? Because too many students wandering about the classroom distracts others from working and can be dangerous. *Why* should we switch our mobile phones off? Because CrazyFrog ringtones are annoying ... and they disturb the lesson, which isn't fair on the teacher or the other students. It helps to set three blanket rules/ rights at the start of the year, which can cover all misdemeanours and are easy to refer to, helping to bring the boundaries of acceptable behaviour into the class mindset. For example:

In this classroom, staff and students have:
- The RIGHT to respect.
- The RIGHT to learn/to teach.
- The RIGHT to feel safe.

It is also useful to display these rules/rights clearly within the classroom, and spend some time discussing why they are necessary, and how the students will benefit from them. To be effective, they also need to be applied consistently. If we only use the rules *sometimes* for *some* students, we are likely to cause a considerable amount of (justified) resentment amongst the class. Frustratingly, this can also be an issue across the school. If some teachers adhere to certain school policies and rules (e.g., not wearing baseball caps and hoods indoors) and others don't, students may become antagonistic towards those who do, and will try to manipulate the system. The answer? Stick together. Whole school expectations, consistently applied, are what work best.

BULLYING

Bullying should always be taken seriously, as its effects can be grave. It is important that you are familiar with your school's policies and procedures on dealing with it, and that if you are unsatisfied with the action that is taken, you lobby to get it improved. It can occur in many forms in and around school – in groups, on individuals, temporary, or long-term – and can have different guises: name calling, threatening, ignoring, ridiculing or physical attacks. There is no question that it can make the victim's life a misery.

Schools vary in the way that they tackle bullying, but it seems that they are becoming increasingly aware of the need to take action. If you are concerned that any of your students are being targeted, you will need to open up a dialogue with them and gain their trust. Offer to talk after school or at break-time, or at least when no other students/possible bullies are listening in. Reassure the student(s) that you will take the matter seriously and give a clear explanation as to how you will be addressing the issue. Bullying interventions vary, and some are considered to be more effective than others:

- *Student meetings.* A group of students meet, including bullies and non-bullies, who may have witnessed the incidents. With the help of a teacher, they discuss how the victim may be feeling and look to find a solution. They reconvene a week later to see what effect it has had. Generally viewed as a 'no-blame' option, this practice has come into criticism for not condemning bullying behaviour.
- *Counselling/mediation.* Managed discussion with a school counsellor/ mediator, in which the victim is encouraged to explain to the bully how their behaviour has affected them. This can, however, be an intimidating experience for the victim, and may just lead to further harassment.
- *Circle time.* This is regularly used in primary school, to encourage students to discuss their feelings, take turns, develop positive relationships, and air problems. It has the potential, however, to be rather humiliating.

- *Peer-group programmes.* Systems such as buddies, restorative justice and peer mediation can be very effective. However students need to be given thorough training and support in order for them to be successful.
- *'Telling' schools.* Increasingly schools are claiming that they have a zero-tolerance approach to bullying, and are encouraging all students to see it as their duty to come forward about incidents of bullying (which helps to protect victims that are too afraid to come forward themselves). This can be very effective as it promotes a whole-school, collective disapproval of bullying behaviour.

IS FOR...

CAUSE AND EFFECT

We all understand that if we compliment someone, it will make them feel good. If we say something mean, it may make them feel bad: the cause and effect principle. But how many of our students seem to stumble down a pathway of disruptive behaviour, despite causing lots of upset to themselves and the people around them, and then do it all again the next day. Either they cannot help themselves, they fail to understand that their actions have implications, or they understand and do it anyway.

Do we live in a callous, uncaring society, where people just do as they please without considering others? Well, maybe. But one of the key problems, especially for students with behavioural difficulties, is acting/reacting before thinking. These individuals tend to see things in fixed 'black and white' terms, and, particularly if they are angry or wound up, will lock onto a certain agenda, whether that is revenge, showing off, destruction or escape. This is something we all experience: think of the last time you were really angry, and said/did something you regretted. Hopefully, however, that sense of regret deterred you from doing it again.

For some, the cause and effect principle is hard to learn, or difficult to keep in mind when caught in the heat of the moment. Here are some suggestions on how you can support these individuals to make wise choices and take responsibility for their actions:

1. *Encourage them to pause.* If you see a student getting 'worked up', intervene in a low-level manner and gently remind them to slow down, and take a moment to think before they react.
2. *Give them some strategies for calming down.* Moving away from the problem. Taking time-out. Deep breathing. Reciting a favourite song. Or the classic: counting to ten.
3. *Use a cue card.* A laminated sheet with step-by-step reminders saying: 'Are you feeling wound up? Stop. Keep calm. Think it through, then decide what to do', which can be stuck on a wall, or on an individual's desk.
4. *Encourage empathy.* Ask students how they would feel if whatever they were doing or about to do was done to them.

CHOICE

For some teachers, the idea of giving students choice over what they do may seem too soft. Surely we lay down the law and they follow it ... or else. But how many of us have been in a situation where we cannot get a child to cooperate, no matter how much we order them about? The fact is we cannot force our students into doing anything they don't want to do (especially if that force takes the form of aggressive or even violent behaviour). The alternative, and by far the more effective method, is to help them decide for themselves that they do or don't want to follow a certain course of action. And we can do this through giving them choices. Compare these two examples:

Gary, one of your most difficult students, has walked into class with an open can of drink. He sits at his desk, clearly not ready for work, and continues to drink from it.

Example A
    TEACHER: *Gary, this is not a café. Throw that drink away now!*
    GARY: *No way! I paid for this, sir. And I'm gonna drink it all ...*
    TEACHER: *No you're not. You're not allowed to drink in class, so throw it in the bin. NOW!*

Gary continues to drink, unbothered.
TEACHER: I'm waiting.
GARY: I'M NOT THROWING IT AWAY! Do you get me? You can't make me. It's mine.
The teacher tries to snatch it off him, which aggravates Gary even more.
GARY: GET OFF ME YOU WEIRDO!!
TEACHER: Right! That's it! Leave the room!

Example B
TEACHER: Gary, you know you're not allowed canned drinks in class. It needs to go away.
GARY: No way! I paid for this. I'm not wasting my money.
TEACHER: I understand that – but the fact is, we have a clear rule about eating and drinking in class. Either you throw the drink away, or you give it to me, and I'll look after it until breaktime. It's your choice.
GARY: It'll be flat by then!
TEACHER: But that's better than having to throw it away completely isn't it? If you go and put it on my desk now, and then get on with the lesson, it will be there for you at the end.
Gary reluctantly places the drink on the desk, and sits back down.
TEACHER: Thank you Gary, that was a mature decision.

Choice gives a wound-up student breathing room. They are less likely to feel cornered, and therefore less likely to get more wound up, helping to minimize stress and de-escalate tension. Importantly, choice also encourages them to take responsibility for their actions – *they* decide what happens. If it all goes wrong, they are the ones that are answerable. If it all goes right, they can feel proud – always praise students for making good choices.

The language of choice may not be something that comes to us naturally, but with practice (for ideas see section on 'Useful phrases'), it can eventually feel perfectly familiar, and become a normal part of our teaching repartee. With it comes a decrease in classroom stress and a decrease in the number of teacher/student 'arguments', which leaves more time for teaching and learning. Two rules, however: keep the choices simple, and don't get drawn into lengthy negotiations. If necessary, remind the student of their options then move away.

CLOTHING

Why is it that the students who cause the most disruption often seem to be the ones who wear trainers instead of shoes, sports jackets instead of the correct school jumper, and baseball caps instead of short, neat hair? The uniform-chase-up game will be familiar to many of us: they wear 'illegal' hoop earrings to class. We tell them to take them off. The next day, they wear hoop earrings to class. We tell them to take them off … and so it goes on.

Young people cling tightly to their fashion beliefs. We live in a world where the wrong clothes can mean social isolation and humiliation, so it is hardly surprising that the request to remove all non-regulation clothing is often met with resistance. Although, as professionals, we are obliged to uphold school policies on uniform, it is sometimes worth reminding ourselves of what our students are up against. They are continuously bombarded with media messages about image and identity, and whether they are wanting to fit in (the 'cliques' with their matching hairstyles) or stand out (the indie kids with purple hair), what the world sees them wearing matters a great deal. In theory, uniform is supposed to remove the threat of judgement on the basis of an individual's clothing choices, but it is a thin disguise. The very ones that uniform is trying to protect will be caught in the end, given away by the fact that their trousers are too short or their skirt is too long. For the image-conscious, there will always be a way to flaunt the rules, and they will always find it. So we, for our part, are consigned to daily struggles with caps and trainers.

CONFISCATION

It is amazing really. So many students struggle to remember their books/pens/calculators/homework, yet they *never* forget the mobile phone, iPod and fizzy drink! The use, or misuse, of inappropriate items in the classroom can cause teachers acres of frustration – the more we press for these things to be put away, the more our students insist that a) music helps them concentrate, b) the fizzy drink calms them down, and c) their mum gives written permission for the phone to be ON. The most effective way of dealing with this issue is through a strong, whole-school approach that all staff adhere to. Within the confines of our own classroom, however, it is possible to manage it without wasting too much time or effort. Try these suggestions:

1. *A clear classroom policy.* Discuss the issue with students at the start of the year/term, explaining exactly *why* such decisions are necessary. If they feel like they have been part of the negotiations, and are encouraged not to see the rules as 'pointless', they will be more likely to respect them (and you).

2. *A sweep at the start.* Although this can be time-consuming initially, I have found the use of a safety deposit box helpful. I collect in students' contraband at the start of the lesson, on the understanding that they will get it back at the end. At first they tend to be resistant to the idea, but I sell it to them on the basis that their valuable stuff will be kept safe, and they end up liking it. No more interruptions, and it also creates opportunities to interact with students at the beginning/end of lessons.

3. *Never snatch.* Frustrated though you may be, never try to forcibly take an item from a student – it will lead to conflict, and could potentially back-fire on you. Instead …

4. *Use choice.* If you calmly give a student options as to what they can do with their item (e.g., 'You can either put the phone back into your bag for the rest of the lesson, or you can put it in my desk and I'll look after it – but I don't want to see or hear it') and allow a little time for them to quietly make the choice, you will solve the problem with much less bother.

5. *Keep it low-level.* Rather than spend precious minutes arguing about chewing gum, comb the aisles holding a bin/ piece of paper, on which students can deposit their gum – no questions asked. The visual cue should be enough, allowing you to continue talking about the lesson.

CONSEQUENCES

Structure should be the bedrock of any behaviour management plan, and a simple way of creating it is through having systems of reward and consequence. In this section we will focus on consequences (for the former, see section on 'Rewards'). Firstly, it is necessary to point out that, although such systems are an aid to behaviour management, they are not a substitute. They will not do the hard work for us (in other words, the 'thinking', the forming of relationships and the preparation) and cannot guarantee that our students will comply with every request we make.

Consequences (or sanctions), in particular, have their limitations. How many of the most difficult students in our schools have been that way for years? How often does challenging behaviour occur and then reoccur? Clearly, sanctions are not the deterrent we would wish them to be. That said, they can be a useful way of showing that actions have consequences, and will also demonstrate, in the eyes of the rest of the class, that justice has been done. Here are some suggestions on how to make consequences effective:

1.   *Be swift.* As with rewards, consequences have most impact when they are delivered quickly after the event (so that the connection between the two is obvious). If you can do it there and then (e.g., keep a student back after class), you will make the point and not have to risk students failing to turn up to detentions.

2.   *Make them fair.* Ensure that the level of sanction matches the seriousness of the crime. If you fail on this count, your students will either resent you or think you're a soft touch.

3.   *Use a menu.* It may be helpful to establish a menu of sanctions that can be displayed in the classroom (alongside a corresponding list of rewards), encouraging consistency and regularity. This could include: withdrawal of privileges, detentions of various lengths (see section on 'Detentions'), phone-calls/messages home, referral to another teacher.

4.   *Keep them simple.* The last thing you need is to waste your time trying to enforce sanctions that are unrealistic. If you are prone to heat of the moment outbursts of 'Right! Detention every night this week!', either learn to control

yourself, or defer your decision ('I'll speak to you about your behaviour at the end of the lesson.')

5. *See them through*. If you wish to maintain credibility in the classroom, be true to your word and avoid making threats that you know you'll never follow through. Say what you mean, and mean what you say.

6. *Work as a team*. Some teachers work together, temporarily 'exchanging' students who are causing problems in their lessons. Also, if you hold regular detentions after school/ break-times, you could take turns being responsible for running these.

7. *Don't punish many for the crimes of the few*. Whole-class detentions, because some students were mucking about, are usually viewed as cruel and unfair, and will cause resentment.

CONSISTENCY

Unfortunately there is no way round this one. If we want to make a long-term, meaningful impression on the behaviour of our students, we need to deal with it continuously and consistently. This will help us to establish boundaries and generate respect. In other words, students will see that we are reliable, fair and unlikely to let them get away with it. We can make it easier for ourselves to maintain consistency by being clear about what it is we do and don't want in our classroom, so it is worth spending some time thinking about this, in terms of what is necessary and what is realistic. It is also helpful to have a clear idea of what happens when things go wrong – to have a 'menu' of rewards and consequences that are easily applied and can be made explicit to our students. (For more guidance see sections on 'Boundaries', 'Consequences' and 'Reward systems'.)

COPING

Everyone has different methods of coping with the stresses of the classroom – some more effective than others. Teaching is a demanding job anyway, but having to deal with tough classes and challenging behaviour can create a lot of additional pressure (see section on 'Hidden fears' for more insight). The effects of stress can be very harmful to our physical and emotional health, and can interfere with our classroom performance, so it is important that we keep them in check. Here are some suggestions:

- NEVER, EVER TAKE THINGS PERSONALLY. It is not worth it. If you are in the firing line, keep reminding yourself that you are going home to your lovely life, friends and family. Whereas your students …
- Don't be afraid to ask for support, whether from colleagues, managers, family and friends, or even counselling services.
- Take proper breaks in the day and learn to say no to excessive demands.
- Look after your health. Teaching requires stamina, so physical activity and a balanced diet can make a difference. Exercise is also a fantastic stress buster.
- Keep hydrated – always have a bottle of water available by your desk, and take regular sips through the day (this will also help to protect your voice).
- Be prepared, but be flexible. Managing a classroom is easier when you are organized and know what you want, but if you are too rigid, you may just be creating more frustration for yourself.
- Listen to your body and rest when you need to. Don't plough on if you are feeling ill or run-down. And don't feel guilty about it.
- Build relaxation into your week. Whatever works for you: self-hypnosis, yoga, watching television, walking the dog. View it as a right, not a treat!
- Make your classroom an oasis of calm – spend a bit of time at the start of each lesson, playing relaxing music, doing brain-gym or guided meditation with your students.
- During times of pressure, do what is essential – ignore what isn't.

CORRIDOR BEHAVIOUR

You are rushing from one end of the school to the other, hoping to squeeze a million priority tasks into one half hour of non-contact time, when you stumble across a group of misplaced students who are loitering in the corridors and looking decidedly suspicious. Do you:

a) Give them the hard-line and march them down to the office, where you personally see to it that they are 'dealt with' and returned to their classrooms – never mind non-contact.

b) Spend ten awkward minutes arguing over who they are and where they should be, knowing you are being taking for a fool, before walking away in frustration.

c) Calmly enquire about where they should be, taking subtle note of their appearance, year group and location, then go and inform a senior teacher.

d) Walk in the opposite direction, hoping they haven't noticed you ...

The fact is, what happens in our classrooms can be affected by what we do around school. For example, if we take the trouble to greet students in the corridor and have a chat or a joke with them, we will strengthen our positive image. And if we are seen to be dealing with inappropriate corridor/playground behaviour – even though they may not be *our* students in *our* classrooms – we are strengthening our reputations as teachers who will not stand for nonsense. (For this reason, I would suggest avoiding option d.) Keep your interventions low-level, as, unless you are 100 per cent confident that the students will be suitably fearful of you, an aggressive manner may lead to conflict (I have seen it happen) – which will then take up more of your time. Firm, calm instructions may prompt them into getting to class, but if not, try this bit of speech:

'Like you, I need to be somewhere else right now, so I don't have the time to argue about this. However, I'm not prepared to just leave you here, as it is against school policy. So either you get to class straight away, or I'll have to inform a senior teacher, and they will deal with you.'

Obviously, this scenario is so much easier to manage if you have prior knowledge of who the students are and where they should be – which unfortunately is not always the case. If you ask for their names, they may give you false ones, but it is usually possible to tell the year group from size or uniform – and the chances are, if they have difficult behaviour, their Head of Year will be able to identify them. In terms of where they should be, you have the option of actually escorting them back to their classes, but this can be difficult and time-consuming if the school is large, or they are in different lessons around the building. Some schools have a facility to which stray students can be sent, which is much easier. If the students refuse to cooperate or there is any sense of foul play, it may be necessary to bring it to the attention of a senior teacher, who can then take over. Ultimately, if senior teachers/management have a strong visual presence around the school and the corridors, such incidences are more likely to be brought under control.

COVER LESSONS

Covering another teacher's lesson is a notoriously grey and difficult area. Unfortunately it is something we have to tackle, sometimes on a weekly, or even daily basis. The reasons why covers are so difficult are obvious:

- The students may not be expecting you and will be unsettled by the change.
- The students may have a good relationship with their main teacher/are enjoying the work, therefore may be disappointed if this cannot be continued.
- The students may have a bad relationship with their main teacher, and/or may not be used to cooperating and following instructions.
- You may not have been given adequate information or lesson plans/work for the class.
- You may not know any of the students/have not had the chance to build a rapport with them.
- Your use of sanctions may be limited, due to not seeing the class consistently.

- The students see it as an opportunity to have an 'easy' lesson.
- The students it as an opportunity to have fun winding the teacher up.
- You see it as a waste of time/are unmotivated by teaching a one-off lesson to a group of students who aren't interested anyway ...

(The same issues can apply to supply teaching, although you may be given the chance to provide long-term cover, which, if you assert yourself, allows you to establish a relationship with your students and get over these hurdles.)

The reality is that cover lessons will always pose a challenge. For this reason, some would argue that it's simply not worth bothering – just stumble through the experience, then walk away without looking back. To a certain point, I agree: why go hell-for-leather for something that amounts to little more than an inconvenience? However, I also believe that what we do around school can have as much impact on our reputation as what we do in our classrooms. The reputation we obtain through interacting with different students throughout the day can spread to the unlikeliest of places. The impression we make on the first year students in today's cover lesson may benefit us when they turn up in our classroom two years later. Alas, there is no magic wand for making cover lessons simple, but I would suggest a few key ideas:

1. Keep a folder of general emergency worksheets/tasks, in case of adequate work not being set – things that are fun and fairly easy, and will therefore hold their interest for a reasonable length of time.
2. Where possible, control the manner in which they first come into the classroom, allowing four or five students in at a time.
3. Assert your firm manner on them at the beginning, just as you would with your normal class and then say something like: 'For those of you who don't know me, I expect a high standard of behaviour during class, *but* I can be a very reasonable person when students cooperate

with me – so this could be a nice lesson for you if you …'
Emphasize the fact that although this may not be what
their normal teacher does/says, this is how it is going to
be whilst you are in charge of the lesson.

4.   Give them a carrot. For example, 40 minutes of calm and
      quiet can lead to 10 minutes' relaxation at the end.

5.   Avoid general threats such as keeping them in at break/
      lunchtime – you will have nowhere else to go. Try using
      a system of consequence: 1 minute for the first mis-
      demeanour, 2 minutes for the second, etc. until they
      reach 5 minutes, for which their names will be referred
      to a senior teacher.

6.   Tell them that the Deputy Head/scariest teacher in the
      school is in a room down the corridor and will come in if
      the room gets too noisy!

7.   Write down all the names of the students who are getting
      on with their work quietly, and explain that you will be
      passing the list on to their teacher/tutor, so that they can
      be rewarded.

DE-ESCALATION

In any situation of conflict or anger, for example, a disagreement between students or a student reacting badly to our expectations, the priority should be to stabilize the atmosphere and restore calm. However tempting it may be to shout at a student or argue back (especially when they are deliberately trying to wind us up), such reactions will only inflame their emotions and lead to further tension. Instead, we need to focus on de-escalating the situation, through our actions and our approach, therefore preventing lasting damage.

The first thing we need to consider is that anger and frustration are universal feelings, and are perfectly legitimate. We all experience them – it is how we express them that makes the difference. I believe that what happens in a classroom is about what the student brings, and what the teacher brings. If both parties are having a 'bad day', the effects can be disastrous. But although we may not have control of our student's issues and emotions, we are able to control ours – behaviour management is as much about managing our own thoughts and actions, as it is those of our students (see section on 'Coping'). Once we are over this hurdle, there are many things we can do to help de-escalate a crisis:

- Approaching students positively, with a quiet voice, eye-control and calm mannerisms.
- Getting as close to the situation as possible, without invading the student's personal space – in times of stress they may need a lot of it, so if they shuffle away from you, don't see this as a cue to move even closer.
- Keeping physical gestures small, open and close to the body (avoiding aggressive 'messages' such as folded arms or finger-pointing).
- Giving clear, simple instructions and focusing on the immediate behaviour rather than what has happened before (i.e., address the anger rather than the whys and wherefores of what they have been doing wrong – that can come later, when they are calm).
- Using empathy to establish trust: 'I can see that you are frustrated by this …'
- Using positive reinforcement and reassurance: 'Do you remember last week how you managed to calm yourself down and get on with the lesson? You did so well, and I know you can do it again. I will help you, but you need to stop shouting.'
- Giving them a 'way out', using choice: 'Either you come and sit over here, or you will leave the room and take some time-out.'
- Distracting students by leading them to another activity, showing them something, or starting up a conversation about something they like (most effective for younger ones).
- Avoiding entanglement by being businesslike and moving away from argument – saying you will happily talk to them when they are calm.

DEFIANCE

Defiance, or refusal to cooperate, should be considered one of the most serious behavioural offences, because its persistence can threaten to undermine our entire behaviour management structure. It is also a very difficult issue to deal with. Our automatic instincts may tell us that if someone is resisting our instructions, we should pressure them even further, until they cave in. But in actual fact, this just makes the person want to resist more – it becomes a power struggle. Consider this scenario:

> *After some unacceptable behaviour, the teacher has asked Kevin to leave the room, but he is refusing to get up from his seat.*
> *TEACHER: Kevin. I've asked you to leave. Will you go please.*
> *KEVIN: Tch … why should I?*
> *TEACHER: Because you've been mucking around and spoiling the lesson, so you need to go.*
> *KEVIN: I'm not gonna. I want to stay here.*
> *TEACHER: I'm not arguing with you about it Kevin. Just go, will you?*
> *KEVIN: No! I AIN'T GOING ANYWHERE! Leave me alone …*
> *TEACHER: I've told you to go … look you're wasting everyone's time. So just go. NOW!*
> *KEVIN: Make me!*
> *And so on …*

As you can see, each party is getting increasingly wound up by the other one's insistence that they are going to have their way. The teacher does the right thing initially, by remaining calm and sticking to the plan, but jeopardizes this by getting locked into the argument and making negative remarks ('you're wasting everyone's time' which may easily be read as 'I am a waste of time', which will only heighten Kevin's aggravation).

Refusal is about control, which is something that people don't like to give up easily. We don't want to be perceived as weak or failing because we cannot 'win' the situation. However, as teachers, we are not in a position to force our students to do anything they don't want to do – we have our professional dignity to keep intact, and besides, arguing is time-consuming. If we find ourselves in a situation like the above, the thing to do is step down. This is not a sign of weakness, but a sign of strength and emotional intelligence. We are recognizing that success doesn't depend on us imposing ourselves on the student, but on resolving the issue calmly and peacefully.

When addressing defiant behaviour, use the language of choice (see sections on 'Choice' and 'Useful phrases'), which will diffuse the power struggle and give the student a way out. And allow for some take-up time – in other words, give the student their options and then walk away. This will allow them breathing space to calm down, and will also take the heat off them if they are playing up to an audience. Some students will then make their choice quietly, whilst others may need a further reminder.

DELIBERATE MISBEHAVIOUR

There is nothing more infuriating than dealing with a student who is deliberately trying to wind you up. Sneaky comments. Answering back. Doing things that they hope will press all your wrong buttons. You know that they know *exactly* what they are doing. Do they get a kick out of it? Is it fun? Are they just showing off? Or are they being malicious? Whatever their intentions, it can be draining and demoralizing. When you sense that such deliberate winding-up is occurring, the important thing is not to rise to it. Maintain an air of neutral disinterest and move away. I also believe it is important to be explicit with students, to talk through their behaviours and possible feelings, which implies that you are trying to understand them, but can also help them to understand themselves. Be discreet and talk to them on a personal level:

'Carly, I realize you are trying to aggravate me. I'm not quite sure why. I don't know whether you might be angry or upset with me, or with someone else. If you are, then I will happily talk about it. I'll try to resolve things with you, but this sort of behaviour is not going to have the effect you want. Let's get on with the lesson shall we, and if you want to talk to me about anything you just let me know …'

Responding in this way diffuses the tension between the teacher and the student, and opens up a dialogue. The teacher has shown that they are not going to be bothered by Carly's attempts to provoke, but has also offered an olive branch. They have explained that they are willing to listen, and even to accept that Carly may be annoyed with them. Maybe it goes against our instincts to try to 'befriend' those who want to humble us, but if we can be the bigger person, who ends up feeling humble?

DENIAL

If you have ever had problems eliciting the truth from your students, you are not alone. Denial of wrongdoing is irritatingly common and can be tricky to resolve, especially if the culprits flatly refuse to own up to behaviour you have *seen* them commit. And of course, there are always those grey areas: did you really see them do it or are you making an assumption based on the fact that they are *likely* to have done it? Can you take one student's word against another? Do you have proof that the calculators that have gone missing were there at the start of the lesson? And what if your enquiries are met with a wall of silence? Here are some suggestions on how to get to the truth:

1. *Divide and conquer.* If you are dealing with a group of students, try to get them separated (where they cannot confer) and then talk to them one by one, asking for their version of events. You may need help from other staff to do this effectively. Then get them together at the end, to 'conference' your findings.

2. *If you are sure …* Take the student outside of the classroom (away from the audience), and ask them in a calm, positive tone, whether they were involved – act concerned rather than angry, or use a casual, 'good cop' approach. If you give them chance to confess, rather than accuse them from the start, you will minimize the risk of denial and confrontation.

3. *'From my perspective …'* If they deny rather than confess their actions, tell them you accept their point of view, but that from your perspective you saw them do X, Y and Z. Explain that they have another chance to admit it to you, or you will have to inform a senior teacher/tutor/parent.

4. *If you aren't sure …* Be honest. Explain that you aren't certain, and that you would appreciate their help in solving the matter – that honesty will be rewarded with a more

lenient sanction. Also, warn them that if no one admits to the behaviour, you will continue your investigation and should you find out that anyone has been lying, the consequences will be serious.

5. *Encourage discussion about responsibilities.* Use PSHCE to explore issues surrounding lying – why people do it, what the consequences are and about the importance of taking responsibility for our actions. A useful sanction for liars is to have them do a 'truth-telling' workshop, where they can discuss and take part in role-play activities.

DETENTIONS

Whenever I run behaviour management training days, the issue of detentions always causes some controversy. Opinion appears to be divided over whether they are effective or not. Some teachers feel they are the only bargaining point they have with their students; others feel that they are a waste of time (theirs and their students'). Therefore, I have divided this section into two parts:

Things that make detentions effective:

- Keeping them short and as close to the incident as possible (i.e., straight after the lesson).
- Holding students through break-times or lunchtimes can be easier to organize and may have more impact on the students as it disrupts their social time.
- Working with other teachers to run detentions on alternate days can relieve the time pressures and shows the students that staff stick together.
- Using the time to have a reflective discussion about the behaviour, writing a sorry letter, or filling in a 'what I did wrong' form.
- Expecting a formal manner within the detention (i.e., correct uniform, sitting in silence).
- Using the time to catch up on classwork – some students will do more work in a detention than during the rest of the year.

- Systems can help – for instance, if a student fails to turn up to a detention, the teacher can fill out a form, which is then taken up by a senior teacher (with a copy sent to the parents), who then chases up the matter with the student.
- Different levels of detention (e.g., short, long, informal, formal, headteacher's) can help reflect different levels of behaviour, and the sliding scale means there is always a next step.

Things that make detentions ineffective:

- Students may avoid turning up to detentions if they are held later in the day/week rather than immediately after the lesson (which is inevitable during some lessons).
- Other teachers will get annoyed if students are frequently turning up late to their lessons, because they have been kept behind by you.
- Keeping some students in at break-time or lunchtime can be counterproductive, if they are the sort that need to 'let off steam' in the playground.
- Overuse can mean they lose their impact.
- Detentions can sometimes involve a lot of chasing up and parents will need to be contacted if they are over 20 minutes – some students are very savvy about their rights and will point this out to you.
- They can cause argument: 'why are you keeping me back and not him?', and some students will always have an excuse: 'I'm captain of the football team and I've got to train tonight'.
- They can end up taking up a lot of your time, and are an added pressure if you are feeling tired.
- If the time is used unconstructively, to relax and have a casual chat, they can become more pleasurable for the student than 'painful' – which defeats the object.
- The most disruptive students aren't bothered by them anyway.

DiFFEREИTiATioИ

A significant contributor to positive classroom behaviour is whether the learning opportunities on offer are interesting, accessible and suitably challenging. If our students are engaged with what is going on in the lesson, they are less likely to be drawn into disruptive, anti-social activity. So the question is, how do we get their attention – and then hold on to it? Some ideas are available in 'Learning styles' and 'Kinaesthetic learning', but this section is concerned primarily with that all-important buzzword: differentiation.

Effective differentiation starts with knowing where our students are at, and in this respect, assessment is a key tool. Unfortunately, student assessment seems to have become rather regimented and laborious over the years, more an aide to government statistics than classroom practice. However, this should not detract from the valuable insight that our own assessment procedures can give us, helping us to create purposeful learning environments and charting progress. I always begin a new half-term with a few tasks that allow me to check on student understanding and skill level, and use the results of these to inform my planning. If I know what my students are capable of or where they may be struggling, I can tailor the work to make sure that my expectations of them are realistic – helping to counteract any resistance or fear that they may fail.

I have seen far too many students waste lesson time misbehaving, because of the unsuitability of the class work. They are expected to complete a written worksheet independently – but they are unable to read and write! I realize that widely varying student ability can create enormous pressures for teachers, as can the fact that some students impact the problem with poor attendance. In an ideal world, classroom sizes would be *much* smaller, allowing for more individualized attention, and the curriculum would provide more flexibility ... but since we have to face reality, here are some small suggestions that will enhance the learning of students with low ability:

- Provide plenty of visual resources (images, objects, video), to support, or as an alternative to, written text.

- If using worksheets: avoid large amounts of written text, and bring them to life with images, key phrases and vocabulary in bold, large font size, cartoon style speech/thought bubbles.

- Is reading/writing always required? Can students present their knowledge through discussion, drawing or demonstration?

- Support literacy skills by providing key vocabulary (on the board or as a handout), lists of frequently used words, wide-ruled exercise books/guidelines, writing frameworks (to help with planning, structure and organization of work).

- Give students clear, simple instructions/lesson objectives, and put a reminder on the board for those who have trouble keeping track.

- Provide specific targets of how much work you expect a student to achieve within a particular time-frame (e.g., two paragraphs in 20 minutes). Ensure that these reflect the ability of the individuals.

- Keep activities short (aiding limited concentration spans – the average person can last for about 20 minutes!). Look at ways to divide up the lesson into three/four sections: a beginning, main task and plenary or whole-class discussion, independent work and feedback.

- Use ICT where possible – it can have a very motivating effect.

- Lots of praise, encouragement and reward.

E IS FOR...

EMOTIONAL LITERACY

One of the main obstacles for young people learning to manage themselves and their behaviour is a lack of understanding of their own emotions. We all experience different feelings – from rage and jealousy to sheer joy. As mature, emotionally rounded adults it is likely that we are able to identify these different feelings within us, and to have an awareness of how they effect our interactions with the world around us. Many young people, however, are yet to reach that level of maturity, and some may never. If, as has been highlighted in the section entitled 'Behaviour', we regard behaviour as the outward manifestation of inward thoughts and feelings, we see that the two things are inextricably linked – confused emotions lead to confused, unpredictable actions.

The idea is simple: if we want students to change their behaviour, we need to help them make sense of their underlying emotional issues, the reasons *why* they may be acting in a particular way. We also need to teach them the value of empathy and understanding others. It is simple in theory, but the reality is complicated. Perhaps such learning should happen in the home, but what if home is where it is going wrong? And is it really our job to cover such personal ground, to be – as some colleagues have put it – social workers, counsellors, personal trainers, role-models and life-coaches all rolled into one? What we can do, at least, is create day-to-day opportunities for students to explore and talk about their feelings, and therefore encourage increased self-awareness. Some suggestions:

- Always be specific when talking about behaviour ('Do not answer back in a silly voice, as it sounds like you are bring rude' rather than 'Do not be silly').
- Use empathy and try to name feelings ('I understand that you might be feeling frustrated/disappointed/annoyed/angry/embarrassed/hurt/etc.').
- Provide students with an opportunity to have their say or give their version of events.
- When discussing a student's behaviour, always encourage them to reflect on why they did what they did. Do this in a positive, non-confrontational way.
- Model your own emotional awareness. If a student has done something wrong, explain how it makes you feel: 'When you talk over the top of me, I feel very frustrated, and because of that frustration, my lessons may become less fun …'
- Consider helping set up a student council/peer support network/'buddy' system, whereby students can develop the skills to support each other.
- Encourage your school to set up anger-management groups, or to invest in the services of a student counsellor.
- Build relationships with your students through banter or chats in the corridor/after class. If you establish trust, they may open up to you/value your opinion.
- If you have concerns about an individual, discreetly approach them and ask if they want to talk – they may not come to you otherwise.
- Let students know that you are someone they can talk to, offer an 'open door' or let them know when and where they can find you.
- If you are inundated with needy students, or are told about problems that are too big for you to handle alone, explain to students that you will support them but that you will need to get the help of a colleague. Never make promises about confidentiality.

EMPATHY

Attempting to see the world through our students' eyes can be very beneficial, not just to them, but to us. Having an awareness of what a person is experiencing enables us to step back and understand – making us more tolerant, more patient and more likely to intervene in a helpful way. It also means that we can know the true root of the behaviour, rather than taking it personally: yes, little Freddy may be calling us every insult he can think of, but are we surprised, given how aggressive his parents are? And why is Louis being so difficult about taking his baseball cap off? Is it because he enjoys arguing with us or because he is worried about his image amongst his peers?

It is important to express this empathy to our students. Explaining to an angry, agitated or upset child that you recognize and understand that they are feeling that way – even suggesting that you would feel that way yourself if you were in their shoes – can have a dramatic, calming effect. Often when students are 'acting out', they are simply looking for someone to notice them, to pay attention to their problems. They may do this in a difficult and sometimes unpleasant way – but before getting wound up, remind yourself that they probably lack the emotional maturity to realize there are alternatives, or are so used to being ignored that shouting loudly/being obnoxious is the only thing that works for them.

EXPECTATIONS

It is easy to fall into the trap of believing that if you have difficult classes you are better off lowering your expectations and then just 'getting through' the year – what is the point in wasting endless time and energy when the students couldn't care less what you do? If you are in this situation, I imagine you are either hoping it will make your life easier, or you are in some sort of despair. If you suspect it is the latter, I would suggest you take some time to heal your battered stress levels, seek advice/support from trusted colleagues and rethink your circumstances. Otherwise, it is impor-tant to recognize that low expectations only reinforce low standards.

The cycle of problematic behaviour will not be broken unless you promote the change, by showing students that you *do* think they can do better and that you *do* think they are capable of achieving.

In other words, you need to have high expectations of your students – no matter how challenging they are – on a whole-class level, on an individual level, on an academic level and on a behavioural level. In *your* mind these expectations can be realistic: you know that this is not the sort of class that will get top grades/ be able to work without any interruptions/will hand in regular homework – it is the little improvements you should be working on. Thinking that you can transform them into perfect, grade-'A' angels is simply setting yourself up to fail. Look at where the class are at now, and where you would like them be – and then focus on gradual progress.

The expectations that you communicate to your students, however, should be high and hopeful. The chances are, these are students that have an ingrained belief that education is 'not for them'. Perhaps they do not see the potential benefits of school (see section on 'Underlying reasons'), or do not have confidence in their learning abilities. They may also be led by the examples around them: 'if he's going to muck about then so am I'. Promoting high expectations will help to redress this attitude: consistently remind them they are worthy of doing the best for themselves, and that you believe they can get there. If you are unfalteringly enthusiastic, it will eventually rub off on them.

FIGHTING

There must be very few teachers who will never in their careers experience the infamous student fight, whether a mass 'rush' in the playground, or an unexpected one-on-one punch up in the classroom. Most fights turn out to be fairly pathetic, but unfortunately there will be those few in which students get seriously hurt, or that become uncontrollable. Perhaps one of the biggest concerns for schools is organized, whole-class/gang fighting, in which large groups of students plan to fight each other at a certain time and place, probably looking to boost their status in the pecking order. On these occasions, unless staff act quickly and intervene *before* anything major happens, fights can be very difficult to control, not to mention damaging to the image of the school. Here are some ideas on how you, as an individual, can help your school to deal with fighting (see also 'De-escalation', 'Physical aggression' and 'Physical intervention'):

1. *Focus on prevention.* If you notice an argument or insults being exchanged this could be a warning sign that a fight is going to start – intervene quickly, directing students away from one another, or keep hold of one and send the other(s) to different classrooms/office(s). It would be prudent to work on resolving the issue between the students, before allowing them to be together again.

2. *Look for body language.* Furrowed brow, tense shoulders, tight fists, flushed face, clenched teeth – these are all indicators that someone is in an aggressive mood and may need some help calming down.

3. *Listen out for rumours.* If anything like a mass fight or 'rushing' (where lots of students jump on top of one person for 'fun') is being planned, there will often be whispers of it circulating round the school. If you pick up on any of this, act quickly. Inform senior staff of what you know, and hopefully they will prevent the action from even starting.

4. *Assess the risk.* If you are alone, do not intervene in a fight yourself, unless you feel it is safe to do so. Most fights require at least two people to ensure that the individuals can be safely separated from one another. Do not put yourself at unnecessary risk (see section on 'Physical intervention').

5. *Send for backup.* This should be your priority. Send a student (one will usually offer to go anyway), make a phone-call or simply call out. You may find that some students are helpful in fight situations, and will, themselves, have a positive influence on getting students apart.

6. *If the students aren't helping* … because they are encouraging the fight and cheering it on, deal with them later and pri-oritize getting staff backup. It usually helps if the crowd of onlookers can be dispersed, but again, you may need extra support to do this.

7. *Think before using restraint.* If you are holding one student, are you making him/her a sitting target for the other one? Remember that two people intervening are always better than one, and that an extra person is also a witness – physical restraint can be very murky water.

8. *Separate immediately.* As soon as you have the students apart, lead them away from one another – one staying with you, and the other going with another teacher, or even a sensible student – where they can no longer see, hear or smell one another. Take statements from each of them and allow tempers to cool before attempting a reconciliation.

9. *Take it seriously.* Any form of aggression, even play fighting or threatening behaviour (including verbal threats), should be viewed in a serious light and properly dealt with. This may mean informing senior staff, parents and even the police, and could/should result in some form of consequence for the culprit, such as fixed-term exclusion.

FOLLOW-UP

Effective behaviour management has three levels: preventative (what to do to avoid problems), reactive (what to do when problems occur) and the follow-up (what to do to make sure problems do not happen again). The principles of follow-up are:

1. *See through threats/consequences.* Whatever you have said you will do, *do* (see sections on 'Consequences' and 'Warnings' for more information). It is vitally important that students do not see you as someone who just threatens but never delivers – a green light to do as they please!

2. *Don't 'forget' about troublemakers.* Whether unintentionally or not, if you send a student out of class for five minutes then leave them there for the whole lesson, you could be making a rod for your own back. They may feel rejected. They may disappear and start bothering another class. They may see it as a way of 'getting out' of work they don't want to do. And, finally, they may be able to avoid taking responsibility for their actions. If you do not have the time to deal with the issue there and then, but cannot face having the student in your lesson, far better to send them to another teacher, where they can be 'looked after'.

3. *The 'conversation'.* Whenever you have had to deal with an incident of challenging behaviour, there will be a point afterwards when you have to address the situation with the student(s). This can be easier and more effective if you have some clear aims. I would suggest these are:

   - Clarifying the facts of the incident.
   - Getting the student to acknowledge their wrongdoing.

- Getting the student to explain why it was wrong (who was affected, etc.)
- Establishing a resolution (what the consequences will be/apologies to be made).
- Talking through what the student could do differently, should it happen again.
- Positive acknowledgement of the student's mature manner/willingness to 'put things right'/future behaviour.

4. *Monitor and acknowledge progress.* If a student's behaviour is improving, let them know that you have noticed and are pleased. Do this discreetly however – although they may be inwardly proud, praise from a teacher can be a dent in a student's street cred, and could have an adverse affect. If poor behaviour is persistent or deteriorates, look out for possible triggers/patterns of activity (see section on 'Triggers').

5. *Share information.* Good communication is one of the keys to a successful school. Do your bit by making sure you pass any relevant or useful information to staff that need to know. For example, if a couple of students have had an argument in one of your lessons, you may want to warn their next teacher that tensions will be running high.

6. *Write it up.* Make sure you are familiar with your school's procedures for documenting any serious incidents, and try to write things up as soon as possible, so that they are fresh in your mind. It does not need to be an essay – just the key facts of when, where, who, what and why. Written evidence (written at the time) forms an important part of the exclusion process, and is useful to impress upon parents.

7. *Be reflective.* No event is wasted if it can be used as a learning opportunity, even if (and sometimes *especially* if) it all goes wrong. Look back over the situation, and reflect on your interventions. What helped? What made things worse?

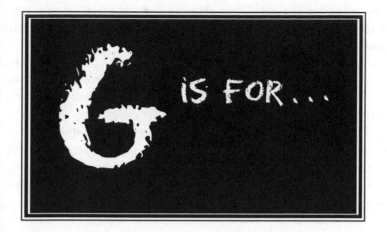

IS FOR . . .

GIVING UP TOO SOON

Many behaviour management strategies are begun with the best of intentions, but then abandoned too quickly, because the member of staff does not see immediate results. The truth is there are no instant fixes for challenging behaviour – especially if this behaviour has become firmly embedded in the attitude and identity of the class/student. This does not mean that strategies will automatically fail, but that they may take time to have the desired effect. The best thing to do if you are embarking on a 'new leaf', or are wanting to try out a particular approach, is to make a consistent effort with it over a half-term period. At the end of this period, if your efforts are working, you should be seeing at least the beginnings of improvement. Stick with it for the rest of the term, and you should find it starts to become habit. If, however, at the end of the half term you have seen no change, or even a deterioration in behaviour, you may need to rethink the strategy or enlist the support of your HofD/senior staff.

Always avoid going down the route of a 'pick and mix' behaviour plan – frequently changing your tactics and your manner. This implies that you are unsure of yourself and your position within the classroom, and can lead to mistrust. As I have stated, strategies may require several repetitions before the students notice them or take them seriously. If they see it happen once, so what. But if they see it happen again, and then again – they get the message. Behaviour management is most effective when it is structured, stable and consistent.

It is also worth bearing in mind that what works for some students in some situations, may not work for others. For example, how you deal with a group of younger students during a drama lesson in the hall may seem patronizing to a group of sixth formers in an ICT room. So within your consistent approach, there needs to be some room for calculated flexibility. And not all strategies have a permanent shelf life – I have seen this happen most commonly with systems of reward and consequence, which become rather too predictable for the students to really care about.

GROUP BEHAVIOUR

Dealing with one disruptive student can be difficult, but having to deal with a group of several – who are all merrily influencing and encouraging each other – poses considerable challenge to our behaviour management skills. It is a challenge that many would like a solution to, but unfortunately there is no simple, quick way of eradicating the problem. Success depends on a number of things, including the relationships we have with our students and the kind of classroom atmosphere we establish – and both of these things have to be worked on continuously in order to have long-lasting and meaningful effect.

Is this a familiar scenario?

The teacher is trying to get the lesson started by explaining the tasks for the session. A couple of girls are talking between themselves, giggling loudly and clearly not listening. The teacher asks them to be quiet, but moments later they start giggling again. Evidently they have got a mobile phone and are sending/receiving silly texts. Just as the teacher goes to intervene, several boys also come over and crowd round the girls' table, wanting to look at the messages. A 'mock' argument between the students ensues, over who gets to see the messages, and eventually one of the original girls jumps up with the phone and runs to the other side of the room. Her friend gets up and follows her, giggling away – and then they are chased by the other students who try to wrestle the phone off them. Throughout this event, the teacher is completely ignored, as if he and his intentions to get the lesson started are completely irrelevant.

The fact is, when students are misbehaving in pairs or groups their power increases – having backup gives them extra bravado, making it harder for the teacher to influence their actions. This phenomenon is not unknown to them either. Although the above scenario outlines a fairly spontaneous series of actions, group behaviour can also be calculated: a deliberate scheme to cause disruption. This is perhaps the most frustrating group behaviour of all, not least of all because its intentions are clearly to upset the teacher … cruel.

Some suggestions on how to tackle coordinated behaviour are covered in the section on 'Unusual noises' (which covers such delights as humming and whistling), but here is a general overview on how to address the misbehaviour of groups of students:

1. *Prevention is better than cure.* The two things you need to focus on are establishing a respectful rapport with your students (see section on 'Relationships') and creating an organized, calm classroom environment with clear routines and expectations (see sections on 'Boundaries', 'Consistency' and 'Routines' … in fact, just read the whole book!). If these things are in place, the likelihood of students trying to 'play' you will decrease. Also, consider seating plans as a way of separating key protagonists.

2. *Intervene early.* Don't wait for a problem to escalate before giving it your attention – but keep it low-level. Show that you are aware of inappropriate activity, by simply moving towards it or using eye-contact – sometimes this is enough to dampen the spark. Otherwise, lean in and have a quiet word, perhaps with a warning that if behaviour continues students will have to move seats.

3. *Get attention.* During a bit of group banter, this can prove extremely difficult. I have watched teachers shout at the top of their voices and still be ignored. Don't get hot and bothered by it – even the most experienced teacher will be ignored if students are suitably 'carried away'. Save yourself the stress of shouting by developing, low-level attention-

gaining tactics (a calm warning, a bell, a 'cue' card) that will
draw in the majority of students, then address the rest of
the class: 'It's such a shame that these students are holding
things up for the rest of you. I appreciate your patience and
I'll make sure you are rewarded for acting sensibly ...'

4. *Focus on the ringleader.* One way to limit the 'power' of
    a group is to remove its nucleus, which is why it is
    important to know your students. If it is not obvious,
    spend some time observing the student dynamics – and
    be aware that leaders are not always the ones with the loud
    mouths (they are often the quieter, bright ones). If you
    can get the ringleader 'on your side' you will benefit. Pre-
    empt a positive relationship with them by giving them
    responsibility (e.g., handing out materials, writing the date
    on the board) or having a positive chat before the lesson.

5. *Divide and conquer.* In the event that group behaviour should
    start to get out of hand, your aim should be to separate
    the troublemakers. In some instances, it is possible just
    to rearrange where students are sat within the room; in
    more serious or persistent difficulties, it may be necessary
    to send students out of the room and into other classes
    – which is where colleague support plays a vital role.
    Some students can be confrontational about being asked
    to move – nevertheless, you are the boss. Inform them
    that if they do not choose to follow your instructions the
    consequences will be more serious, and that senior staff
    may have to be called.

HIDDEN FEARS

Any potentially 'explosive' situation will be met with a certain level of anxiety from those involved. Dealing with challenging behaviour and confrontation in the classroom it is no different. As teachers, we can try to appear confident and sure of ourselves, but there may always be that little bit of doubt in the backs of our minds:

- Will I know what to do?
- Will I be made to look stupid/weak/ineffective?
- Will I be in control?
- Will I cope?
- Will I be safe?

It is not something we often discuss or admit to: some people (wrongly) view fear or anxiety as weakness; but if not given its due attention, this 'fear' can cause an enormous amount of stress. To experience it is perfectly understandable and healthy. If we waded into every situation with blindly heroic bravado we would find ourselves in all kinds of trouble – caution helps us to make wise decisions. It is important, however, that the level of anxiety we experience does not interfere with our ability to deal with the situation rationally and effectively; therefore, we need to find ways of managing these worries:

- *Will I know what to do?* As long as you have taken the trouble to familiarize yourself with your school's behavioural policy, and, if necessary, researched some useful strategies, and are doing what you can to apply these things, you are, at least, doing what you know. With time and experience, you will find you develop an 'instinct' for dealing with situations.
- *Will I be made to look stupid/weak/ineffective?* Yes. They will certainly try. And unfortunately that goes for certain staff members as well as students. The short answer to dealing with it? Don't ever take it personally.
- *Will I be in control?* The answer to this relies on you as an individual. Are you naturally able to remain calm under stress, or could you benefit from some additional help? Experiment with relaxation techniques or develop a personal strategy for being able to keep calm (counting to ten, or deep breathing – see section on 'Coping' for further suggestions).
- *Will I cope?* Again, this is about you as an individual. Are you the sort of person who blames themselves when things go wrong, or can you step back and recognize that sometimes doing everything right is *still* not enough to make the little scamps behave themselves? Humour goes a long way here!
- *Will I be safe?* Although there are no guarantees, if you concentrate on doing what you can to diffuse conflict and maintain a calm atmosphere, you are reducing the risk of violent/dangerous behaviour.

It is also worth remembering that we are not the only ones who may be experiencing fear. Many students, when caught up in confrontation or difficulty, will be put under further pressure from their own personal anxieties: Will I be in control? Will I look stupid? Will I be listened to? Will I be safe? What will happen next? We can help to reduce these anxieties by reacting calmly and consistently, and making sure that we explain things in clear and unambiguous terms.

HOME-LIFE

There is no getting away from the fact that whatever is done to educate and nurture young people whilst they are in school will be conditioned and possibly hindered by what happens to them in their home/personal lives. When it comes to behaviour, the school environment – the teachers and the discipline – is only part of the equation. Other circumstances, be they social, cultural, economic, political or personal, can and often do interfere. Sometimes we may pull out all the stops for an individual student, only to find that our efforts are constantly being undermined, and consequently unravelled, by obstacles such as lazy parenting, bad influences or inappropriate housing.

Although we cannot do much about these things, it is vital that, within reason, we are aware of them. For example, knowing that a child is experiencing a difficulty such as family break-up will increase our sensitivity to their needs and help us to be more 'tolerant' of their challenging behaviour – which may ultimately make a huge difference to their feelings of security and stability. Conversely, if we are the ones to notice any unusual changes in an individual's behaviour, we may be among the first to discover that things are not going well 'at home', and can offer a line of support.

No, we are not social workers, but the teacher's role has an element of pastoral care within it – some take to this more than others. Wherever possible, if we, as education professionals, can create strong links between ourselves and the other agencies that may be involved with a child/young person's welfare (such as social services, youth workers, medical professionals, psychology services and the police), we are at least helping to bridge the gaps. This also includes building relationships with parents and carers. Love them. Hate them. Blame them. Fear them. But the more we can get them on our side, the easier it is to establish consistent boundaries for our students. For further information see section on 'Parents'.

Perhaps we do not have control over what happens in our students' lives beyond the school gates, but for the sake of our sanity, maybe it's just as well! At some point in the day we need to draw a line under our struggles, to leave work at the school gates and go and enjoy our own home-lives.

HUMOUR

A sense of humour can be a valuable asset in the classroom. Not only does it help us to cope with the challenges of the day, enabling us to laugh off comments about our bad hair/screechy voice/ boring lessons, and to see the funny side of disastrous moments, but it can also play a useful role in building a positive rapport with students. A humorous comment can be one of the most effective ways of diffusing a simmering difficulty. It can also be used to enliven lessons and make the classroom experience seem 'fun' and appealing. All of these things can, of course, contribute to improved student behaviour.

There is, however, a level of caution to be exercised. Any humorous comment that may have an element of cruelty or ridicule directed at the students is a no-no. Not only is it professionally dubious, but it may cause resentment amongst the class, creating more problems than it solves. The line between 'good-natured' and 'mockery' can be fairly thin, however. Some teachers create great relationships with their classes through gently taking the Michael out of them – but the chances are, these are well-judged performances: the teachers know their students very well, and their students know them.

If in doubt, concentrate on humour that is self-effacing (Pupil: Miss, your lessons are so boring. Teacher: I knew I shouldn't have skipped those lectures in clown school!). I find saying absurd things often amuses my students – especially when they don't quite know whether I am being serious or not. I once convinced a whole class that I had a private zoo in my back garden – I was forever known as the Zoo-Lady. Lastly, there's nothing wrong with not using humour at all. It can be extremely powerful, but not everyone feels comfortable making jokes or wisecracks, and this does not mean they will automatically be disliked or disrespected.

IS FOR...

IGNORING

From conversations I have had with other teachers, it seems there is nothing more infuriating than the student who refuses to listen. Rude. Selfish. Immature. Time-wasting. Frustrating. Whether you are trying to address a group of students who are carrying on with their own jokes and chat, or trying to get the attention of an individual who is deliberately ignoring you, your buttons are being pressed. In the case of deliberate ignoring, power is the key, and unfortunately all the good cards are in their hands. Here are some suggestions on how to address the issue without losing your rag:

1. *Keep calm.* Remind yourself that if you enter into the power struggle (i.e., show the student that you are getting wound up, or try to argue them into listening properly) you are creating a win/lose situation – and you will probably lose. They are trying to make you look silly/ineffective/weak, so don't rise to their bait.

2. *Use your position.* Avoid shouting across the room to get a student's attention. Move close towards them and get down to their level. It is much harder to ignore someone who is addressing you at close proximity.

3. *State your expectations clearly then stand down.* 'I need you to listen to me, but if you're not ready to do that, I'm not

going to waste the class/my time … I'll come back to you in three minutes, and hopefully you'll be ready then. If not, then there will be consequences, because we have a class rule about being respectful and listening to one another.' Then go and positively interact with the rest of the class. If the student still ignores you when you return to them, put consequence in place (stay in at break/note to tutor/etc.) and leave it at that.

4. *Work on the 'friends'.* If an individual is engaging in conversation with other students when they should be listening to you, it can sometimes help to focus on the other students, who may be more compliant: 'Boys, you're not helping Jamie by talking to him when he is supposed to be listening to me. I know you can be very sensible so please show me by getting on with your own work …'

5. *Positively engage the rest of the class or nearby students.* Rather than address the ignoring student directly, try enthusing the others: 'Right! Who can tell me what the word "radical" means? A merit for the first person to get it right …' Then draw the student in: 'Jamie, do you agree? Or do you think it means something else?' Opening up a dialogue, regardless of what it is about, is a helpful way of sidestepping the ignoring behaviour, and thereby diffusing the tension.

6. *The stuck-record approach.* If students are continuing to talk over you, use a single word ('stop!' or student's name) and repeat it loudly and forcefully, until they are badgered into paying attention to you. This can be very effective, but only works if you are firm and persistent.

7. *Use guilt.* 'I'm sorry that you are choosing to ignore me, because you may end up missing out on some interesting/ useful information – and I don't want to have to tell your mum/dad/tutor that you forgot your manners this morning.'

8. *Reverse psychology.* This can work very well as it often takes a student by surprise: 'I see you're ignoring me. I usually do that when I'm angry with someone. So have I done something to upset you?'

INDIFFERENCE

Perhaps one of the biggest menaces to a young person's education experience is the culture of indifference that haunts our society. I'm not suggesting it is worse now than it used to be, but it seems that the battle to engage students in school life is becoming increasingly complicated. Of course, attitude towards education is linked very closely to aspiration, and whilst there are so many mixed messages being banded about it is no wonder that young people are confused and suspicious of what education can do for them. On the one hand, they are told they will get nowhere without qualifications and degrees, on the other, graduates are finding it increasingly tough to get ahead in the workplace, and employees are complaining of declining standards. Not to mention the painful costs of higher education – yet some students are being paid a weekly wage to stay on post-16. And what happened to learning for learning's sake? Or is it all about job prospects and meeting targets? For young people, it's hard to keep focusing on the future when the here and now is so much more accessible. Music. Fashion. Who's going out with who. And all of this is heartily endorsed by the rise of the popular-culture icons (namely celebrities and *Big Brother* contestants) who encourage us to believe that stupidity is quaint, and that giant boobs and crazy hairstyles are all that is needed to lead a wealthy, glamorous lifestyle … give me strength!

(Rant over.)

INTERRUPTIONS

Imagine you have just got into your lesson flow. The class have settled and are engaging with what you're saying. Aware that they are a group that prefer to be 'doing something' rather than listening for long periods, you are keen to explain the lesson task and get started. But then … two girls arrive late with some weak excuse that they are desperate to explain to you. You swiftly integrate them into the classroom and carry on. It all goes well, then … a senior teacher marches in and removes one of the students for reasons unknown to you. A murmur of curiosity from the rest of the class, then you manage to get them settled again. A few more minutes and … Debbie from 10B comes in to remind her younger brother that he is going to the dentist at lunchtime. Five, slightly more restless minutes, and … Arnold points out that some wandering sixth formers are loitering at your door and pulling faces. You open the door and shoo them away, but one of them tries to barge in and starts threatening a group of boys …

Whatever form an unwelcome intrusion takes, it has the power to destroy the momentum of a lesson, and can corrode the patience levels of you and your students – not to mention the excitement and distraction it can sometimes cause. The frequency of such events depends on the whole-school environment.

- Are reasonable measures taken to deal with student lateness? Are time allowances made between lessons for students to get from A to B? Are teachers being encouraged to release classes on time? Is there a whole-school system of dealing with persistent lateness, e.g., detention?
- As far as possible, are staff allocated their own classroom space? Limiting the occurrence of other teachers 'popping in' to get things.
- Are there clear procedures for communicating with other staff during lesson time? Sending notes. 'Exchanging' difficult students. Using common sense to know when is and isn't a good time to ask for keys/borrow a textbook/ speak to a student. Being able to contact a helpful member of staff should students need removing.
- Are corridors well managed? Management and senior staff monitoring out-of-class activity, and regularly 'combing' the corridors to pick up truants and stragglers. The possibility of their presence may deter some students.
- Is there a 'home' for disruptive students and wanderers? A location or classroom where students can be sent to, where they will be effectively and thoroughly looked after, i.e., not allowed to sit around and share anecdotes and tips on how to wind people up.

In general, if intrusions are a problem for you, deal with them firmly but politely. Avoid risky, though sometimes tempting, strategies such as blocking a door or a student's pathway – which can cause confrontation. If a student makes violent threats, calmly state that you do not accept menacing or threatening behaviour in your classroom, so either they leave quietly or you will call senior staff. Make sure that any threatening remarks are reported and followed up.

If students are making silly interruptions or fooling about to distract your class, aim to address them outside of the classroom (away from the audience) and explain that unfortunately their 'highly amusing' antics are not interesting the class today, because everyone is busy with a really enjoyable lesson – therefore the 'entertainment' is more likely to annoy the class than impress them. Knowing where to then redirect a student/group of students is always going to be difficult, unless there is a specific place they can be sent or you know which lessons they should be in. My experience has been that if they are not properly 're-housed', they will either return to your class or start bothering another one. If necessary contact, or threaten to contact, a senior member of staff who will then (hopefully) deal with them.

Not all intrusions have to be unwelcome, of course. Sometimes a quick chat with a member of staff can provide some light relief, or even entertainment within the lesson. Young people benefit from seeing adults communicating positively with one another, and a bit of banter between yourselves can often bring a lesson to life. I have even known teachers to deliberately orchestrate interruptions from other staff and students, in order to demonstrate/role-play an idea or problem – and often to great comic effect.

JUSTICE

If anyone ever suggests that today's young people do not know their right from wrong, I will argue that the opposite is true. In my experience, young people, including some very challenging individuals, have a very strong sense of what is fair. Justice matters greatly to them. I have seen students react very angrily if they believe that they or one of their classmates are being treated unfairly. Their respect can be quickly lost if they see a teacher regularly meting out unreasonable punishments, or accusing students of things they have not done. Since exchange of respect is one of the most valuable resources of the classroom, it is imperative that teachers do what they can to uphold it. In other words, be fair.

- Ensure that the level of sanction fits the seriousness of the behaviour (see section on Consequences).
- Apply sanctions consistently – don't let favoured students get away with things that others don't.
- That said, be prepared to judge each situation on its own terms – swearing at someone because they deliberately screwed up your work is not the same as swearing at someone for the sake of it.
- This use of judgement is particularly important when dealing with students who are being challenging because they are genuinely upset or angry.

- Share out privileges and responsibilities, allowing different students to have the opportunity each day/week – rather than always offering them to the reliable/well-behaved ones.

- Acknowledge and reward the well-behaved students, but also draw attention to the improvements made by more difficult students.

- If in doubt, *listen* to your students' viewpoints and discuss their perception of what is and is not fair in the classroom.

- Make it clear that *you* have expectations over what is fair for you, i.e., that students should listen, be polite, focus on their work, let you do your job.

- Don't let things slide. As much as students dislike seeing either themselves or one of their mates in trouble, the majority of them hate having teachers who do nothing/very little to address misbehaviour.

KINAESTHETIC LEARNING

A large part of the behaviour management process is about preventative practice – putting things in place that will decrease the chances of problem behaviour occurring in the first place. One way to achieve this is through adapting your approach to teaching and learning, maximizing the chances of engaging students in on-task behaviour. In other words, making your lessons enjoyable and accessible. I realize that many teachers are sick of being told that if they want their classes to behave they need to deliver more 'fun', 'exciting' lessons. We all know that the solution is not that simple. Firstly, if we were to make every lesson that 'fun' we would run ourselves ragged. Secondly, even 'fun' lessons will have limited power over the most hardened, disaffected students. And lastly, well, surely our role is to educate – not entertain! This does not mean, however, that we should not be taking realistic steps towards making learning activities appealing and approachable.

When working with students or classes where challenging behaviour is a concern, the chances are energy levels will be high, academic levels will be low and concentration spans will be short. (Anyone who is having difficulties dealing with poorly behaved high-achievers should also look at sections on 'Learning styles' and 'Pace' for ideas). With that in mind, it is easy to see how a more formal chalk-and-talk/worksheets-in-silence type of lesson can create problems. These individuals need to have their mental and physical energy channelled into practical, participatory activities that grab their attention. This does not imply that work should not be challenging or that more formal tasks such as reading and writing should not be included, but where possible, if tasks can be about 'doing' and 'experiencing', students will benefit. Here are some suggestions for how to make your classroom a more 'kinaesthetic' learning environment:

1. *Use drama.* Role-play is a great way to get students to explore new concepts or issues. Getting students to 'be the teacher', in which role they have to answer questions or solve problems, can be popular. Involving popular TV-show formats is also a winner: try *Countdown* and *Who Wants to be a Millionaire?*

2. *Use objects.* Where possible, artefacts, images and models – that can be physically explored – are a good starting point for engaging student interest. *Google Images* is fantastic for finding pictures, which can then be laminated. Many education authorities have access to resource libraries, from which topic-related artefacts can be borrowed – so there's really no excuse!

3. *Use breaks.* Incorporate planned breaks, or simply slot them in when you sense that the class are getting restless. Keep them short and give them a focus: a stretch, changing seats, standing up after a period of sitting, reorganizing classroom furniture or a relaxation activity.

4. *Use games.* Anything that disguises learning as fun can be useful. If key words/ideas are typed out and laminated they can be sorted, ranked, matched, discussed or used for bingo.

5. *Use language.* Carefully phrased questions can draw students into the learning experience and help them to visualize: How did you feel when … ? If you were … what do you think you would do?

6. *Use practical activities.* Carrying out experiments, using equipment, making models or video presentations – anything that gives students a 'hands-on' experience.

LACK OF EQUIPMENT

A familiar teacher pet-hate is students turning up for lessons without the most basic of equipment such as pens and pencils, let alone the right textbooks or homework. And beyond the fact that such disorganization is frustrating and time-wasting, it alludes to a more worrying background trend: student apathy towards education (see section on 'Indifference'). The implication being: why bother bringing a pen to class when I probably won't do any work anyway? Unfortunately this is an attitudinal thing therefore no amount of nagging and pestering will guarantee all students bring pens to all lessons. Add to this the fact that there is that percentage of students who genuinely have difficulties organizing themselves. Somehow it feels like the role of getting them organized will inevitably fall to us. Here are some suggestions on how to deal with disorganized students, whilst minimizing the damage to your lesson momentum:

1. *Try a sanction/incentive system.* A brief detention for those who forget. A merit/sticker/point for those who remember. Or use a simple tick/cross chart and tell students that the people with the most ticks at the end of the term will get a reward.

2. *Make it a challenge.* You may be able to motivate students to bring equipment if you make a 'fun' big deal of it. I once

used a piece of ribbon to tie a pen to a student's jacket, which he and others found very funny. They reminded me of it every lesson ... and remembered their pens.

3. *Get them to borrow from a friend.* If they have to do this enough times, the friend will eventually get fed up and tell them to get their own. Peer pressure!

4. *Keep a store.* If you want to save having to argue about it, have a collection of pens and other stationery that can be lent out – ensure that everything is collected in at the end of each lesson. If necessary keep a name list.

5. *Keep exercise books in the classroom.* If students take them home there is a good chance they will never come back.

6. *Have a separate homework book/folder.* Or hand out lined paper that can, when returned, be stuck into the student's book or file.

LEARNING STYLES

There has been much discussion and research into learning styles in recent years, and expectations have been laid down for teachers to incorporate it into their lessons. As if we didn't have enough things to worry about! But there are genuine gains to be made from using different types and styles of learning activity. Everyone learns in different ways and at different rates, not to mention the fact that some students get bored very quickly, so the more variety you can bring into your teaching the more chance you have of making the desired impact and holding their attention. Here is a very brief overview of some different learning styles:

- *Interpersonal learners.* Students who like to work with other people and share ideas. They also like explaining things and helping others. Try: group work, pair work, student demonstrations, talks, discussion then feeding back to the class, debates.

- *Intrapersonal learners.* Students who prefer working on their own, like doing things in their own way and dislike distractions. Try: quiet reading, individual work, setting own targets, self-directed projects, personal research.

- *Kinaesthetic learners.* Students who learn through 'doing', and enjoy physical, movement-based activities. Try: drama and role-play, model-making, practical demonstrations, field trips, orienteering, activities that involve movement. See section on 'Kinaesthetic learners' for more suggestions.
- *Visual-spatial learners.* Students who are artistic, like to create things and have visual evidence. Try: providing visual resources (images, artefacts, etc.), spidergrams and charts, visual cues around the classroom (key vocabulary, posters), illustrating work, describing something through drawing, puzzles.
- *Linguistic learners.* Students who enjoy using words, and like reading and writing. Try: word games (crosswords, wordsearches, anagrams), vocabulary tests, reciting their own work, discussions, debates, presentations, creative writing.
- *Logical learners.* Students who want facts, like structure and data, and are often strong mathematicians. Try: examining chart and statistical evidence, emphasizing basic facts, problem-solving activities, step-by-step instructions.

LEAViNG THE CLASSROOM

Students may wilfully decide to leave the classroom for a number of reasons. They may be feeling angry or frustrated. They may be trying to avoid some sort of consequence or duty. Or they may just be 'mucking about'. I am often asked how teachers should stop students who are attempting to run away from them. My answer is don't. I realize how frustrating it is when students avoid taking responsibility for their actions, as they bound off down the corridor laughing with their mates. But, unless we can convince them with words, what other means do we have of getting them to remain in a specified area? Physically restraining them? Not exactly ethical (unless they are a danger to themselves or others). Locking them in? Dubious at best. Blocking their pathway/the door? The latter seems to be the most common reaction, but actually carries considerable risk: what if the student threatens you, shoves into you or even hits out at you? And then accuses you of menacing them? It happens. Chasing after them? It turns the whole thing into a game – one which you are most likely to lose.

If a student is trying to leave, firmly inform them that this will incur consequences, but that if they choose to stay, and maturely face their responsibilities, those consequences will be avoided. The key to making this effective is through ensuring that the consequence for running away from a member of staff is suitably powerful (possibly involving parents and/or senior teachers), and that it is definitely followed through.

Wherever possible, I believe it is important to make students accountable for their own choices and actions, and allowing students the choice as to whether they run away from a specified area or not is a perfect example. Yes. It may be tempting to 'control' the situation, to keep the upper hand by forcing the student to stay and listen to you, but ultimately they could learn a lot more from having the responsibility on their shoulders, plus you can keep your professional dignity intact.

LISTENING

Know that if you have ever had difficulties getting a class to listen to you without (sometimes constant) interruptions, you are not alone. This section deals with the issue of how to get students to listen and pay attention to you at the start of the lesson, or indeed, any time that you need to interrupt them from what they are doing and get them to focus on you. One of the most frequent complaints I hear from teachers goes like this:

'The class come in – it takes them a good five minutes to get sat down, take off their coats, get their books out, etc. Then as soon as I've started to tell them about the lesson, someone comes in late – and starts up a conversation with his mates as he saunters across the classroom. I carry on, and within a minute, another group of students have started chatting to each other. I deal with them, and then someone else starts asking me ridiculous questions about my new car. I warn them that we've got a lot to get through and try to continue, but within five minutes, two of them have started arguing with one another. In the meantime, the ones that have been trying to listen are getting stroppy and bored – and blaming me! Once the lesson is underway, things usually improve – but when I'm trying to explain things at the start, I sometimes feel as if I'm invisible.'

Getting students to pay attention at the start of lesson can be extremely challenging, no matter how experienced a teacher you are. This could be for one of a number of reasons:

1. They have not settled down from break or lunchtime, and are still in 'casual' mode.
2. They have concentrated hard in the previous lesson and have now reached saturation point.
3. They have mucked about during the previous lesson and are still 'high' from that experience.
4. They are testing your mood.
5. They are assuming that the lesson will be boring/too difficult/too easy and are intentionally delaying its delivery.
6. They struggle with extended periods of teacher 'talk' anyway.

With this in mind, we are able to see that sometimes, no matter how much effort we put in, students will be struggling to place themselves in the hoped for frame of mind. So perhaps the first thing we need to consider is how reasonable are our expectations, not just of them, but of ourselves? If we are teaching one of our liveliest groups straight after lunch on Friday afternoon, clearly the amount of settling time is going to be longer than what is needed first thing Monday morning.

Another important consideration is how we are drawing the students into the lesson's themes or activities. From my experience, the quicker I can lead my more lively students into 'doing' things, the better. Instead of introducing the lesson with a bit of talk and explanation, I often dive straight in with an activity – something simple that they will 'get' without too much fuss. I used to start my maths lessons (not my strongest subject) with a few rounds of quick-fire mental arithmetic problems, in which a squidgy ball would be passed around to whoever was answering the question – it eventually became a routine, and added a bit of competitive challenge which the students enjoyed. Once they got used to the routine, they would stop and pay attention as soon as I pulled out the ball!

The element of surprise is another effective way of grabbing student attention. If you can come up with practical ways of introducing a lesson that may provoke or intrigue them, they will want to know more. This can range for dramatic gestures such as putting on a costume or role-playing, to simple things: making a bold statement, or giving them a challenge: 'Who thinks they can make this fizzy drink disappear by the end of the lesson – *without* drinking it?' – a science lesson on evaporation. Here are some further suggestions for gaining or reclaiming student attention:

- Raising your hand, as a signal for everyone to copy you (relies on students becoming familiar with the routine, but can be very effective)
- Making the whole class/individuals stand up until they are quiet and calm again
- A whistle or bell, to signal when the class have become too noisy
- Moving around the room and positioning yourself near noisier students
- Projecting your voice (*not* shouting) – talking from the belly and lowering the tone
- Two claps and a click, which students have to copy (this has been used effectively in primary schools, but may be deemed as patronizing by older students)
- Writing on whiteboard: 'By the time I've finished writing this you will all be quiet!'
- Using a countdown, either verbal or with a visual cue (a stopwatch, egg timer or timer on an interactive whiteboard – if you're lucky enough to have one!)
- Perhaps the ultimate key to gaining student attention, however, is confidence – for all of the different techniques and tactics that can be tried, none of them will make an impact if the teacher lacks a sense of authority (genuine or otherwise).

LOW-LEVEL DISRUPTION

Unless you work in a particularly tough school or have students with Emotional, Social and Behavioural Difficulties (ESBD), it is far more likely that the most common problem to plague your classroom is low-level disruption. Although less serious in its nature than more extreme outbursts of challenging behaviour, low-level activity is nevertheless highly frustrating and potentially one of the most powerful destroyers of positive classroom energy. Types of behaviour could include:

- Calling out across the classroom
- Chatting whilst the teacher is addressing the class
- Chatting 'too much' or 'too loudly' during work time
- Getting out of seats at inappropriate times, or without permission
- Silly, attention-seeking noises (humming, screeching, etc.)
- Inappropriate responses to teacher questions
- Work avoidance
- Lack of basic courtesy
- Hindering other students
- Cheeky or impertinent remarks
- Fidgeting
- Unnecessary non-verbal noise (chair scraping, tapping pens, etc.)
- Infringing class/school rules (inappropriate dress, eating in class, chewing gum, mobile phones, iPods, etc.)
- Verbal banter between students
- Misusing equipment
- Non-directed swearing (i.e. not *at* anybody).

The good news is, if you have a firm handle on low-level behaviours, they are unlikely to escalate into more serious difficulties or loss of classroom control. Make sure that you pick up on them. Don't pretend you haven't noticed the boys swapping football stickers in the back row, whilst quietly hoping that no one else has noticed too – they have, and they'll probably join in. If students see you having a quick, firm reaction to their 'little' attempts to push the boundaries, they'll know that your expectations are high, and will be deterred from pushing the boundaries even further. And if you are persistent in your bid to stem low-level disruption, as the year progresses, it will occur less and less frequently.

Low-level behaviour generally requires a low-level response. In other words, avoid shouting, sending most of the class out or getting hysterical. However, you do need to come across as firm. It is therefore useful to have classroom expectations and rules established clearly in your mind, as well as knowing what backup you have should warnings not be enough (see sections on 'Rewards' and 'Consequences'), helping you to feel sure of yourself. The approach I favour is the no-nonsense, you-should-know-what-I'm-expecting-you-to-do tone, in which I feign surprise if the boundaries are pushed: '*Why* can I still hear talking?'

When you are picking up on every little detail of behaviour, it is likely that students will start to view you as 'strict' – this in itself is not a bad thing, but if they also start to view you as moany or unpleasant, the atmosphere of the classroom will suffer. The way to avoid this is by being 'strict' with the rules, strict with whole-class behaviour and then friendly with individuals. Here are some further suggestions for how to deal with low-level disruption:

1. *Clear expectations from the start.* Always spend time outlining the rules at the start of each year/term. A simplified version or a reminder can also be delivered at the start of each lesson, as students are lining up or settling – be positive and imply that you are looking forward to a good lesson.

2. *Learn names.* Being able to pick someone out by name is far more effective than simply saying 'Oi you'! It also implies a level of respect.

3. *Give warnings.* Give a student the chance to do the right things before serving them a sanction. Two warnings are enough. If you are consistent and see through sanctions where necessary, they will realize that you mean business (see section on 'Warnings').

4. *Use humour.* Some behaviour can be effectively diffused this way, and it helps you to build a rapport with the class (see section on 'Humour').

5. *Be explicit.* Whatever your students are doing wrong or right, make it clear to them – avoid generalizations and vague phrases such as 'Stop being silly!' One person's silly is another person's normal! Get into the habit of defining behaviour as '*who* is doing it', '*what* is being done' and '*why* it is unacceptable'.

6.   *Focus on the positives.* Making a positive example of students doing the right thing allows you to avoid sounding negative and will encourage others. For example, 'Thank you to the students in the middle row, who are showing they are ready to listen – well done!'

IS FOR...

MANAGEMENT

This section deals with the issue of how teachers dealing with challenging behaviour can aim to get the best from their school management teams. I include it because I have so many conversations with teachers who complain that they do not feel they are receiving adequate backup from theirs. Before I offend millions of managers out there, I wish to point out that I have worked in a number of schools, some particularly challenging ones, and have seen a lot of examples of supportive, strong leadership. But I have, like many others, seen my fair share of problems. My intention is not to do a bout of management-bashing, but rather to highlight the benefits and difference that good management can make.

There are two distinct levels of management within a school. Firstly, there are the 'middle' managers, for example, the Head of Year and Head of Department level, who will generally be involved with classroom teaching as well as their management responsibilities. They are in a fairly tough position, with lots of extra work and pressure, but not much extra time or money for their efforts. It is likely that you will have a closer relationship with them than other managers (depending on your position within the school) – they are, essentially, your line managers.

- Recognize the pressures they may be under, and therefore avoid burdening them unnecessarily. If you can sort a problem out yourself, then do so – it looks better to your students as well.
- That said, with serious incidences or with difficulties you are having trouble surmounting, do not hesitate to seek their support – if you can go to them with a view on how you would like them to support you, so much the better. For example, temporarily withdrawing difficult students, spending time in the classroom to help you settle the class at the beginning, chasing up students who have avoided your detentions, giving rewards and certificates, backing you up when dealing with difficult students/parents.
- Take the initiative. If you have ideas that you would like to try, perhaps a new reward system or strategy, talk it through – show that you are willing and keen to make progress, and are not just going to rely on them to deal with problems.
- Keep them informed of any changes or issues within your classes. They will not be able to help you, or the students, if they don't know what is going on.
- Don't be afraid to ask for advice or ideas. There is no shame in wanting to learn from other people or in admitting that you do not have all the answers. They may have a lot of valuable experience to share.
- Respect experience, but don't automatically assume that younger managers (relatively new teachers are increasingly taking up management roles and are hungry for career progression) will not be up to the job.
- Be a good team player. Support your colleagues and support your managers and, in theory, it should all come back to you!
- If you are not receiving the support you need, despite asking, you have several choices: either talk it through with a senior manager (beware of conflict potential), find someone who *will* support you (job descriptions are pretty woolly anyway), do nothing (suffer and get stressed) or leave.
- If you are being bullied by a manager, be assertive and seek the support of someone more senior than them.

Unfortunately bullying amongst staff seems to be rife in some schools, and they are not always proactive in dealing with it – that doesn't mean you don't have to be.

Senior managers, heads and deputies, generally play a different role around school than that of the class teacher. Their teaching commitments will probably be minimal (if any), allowing them to devote time to the day-to-day running of the environment. They are also under enormous pressures, with increasingly complex demands being placed on them. Some will endeavour to remain as close to the immediacy of school life as possible, maintaining a strong 'presence' amongst students and staff. Others will spend their days tinkering with the mechanics from the privacy of their office. In general it seems that the 'gap' between teachers and senior managers can sometimes cause misunderstanding and frustration. In terms of behaviour, the ingredients of successful senior management teams seem to be thus:

- They review, consult and promote the school behaviour policy as frequently as necessary – seeking input from all parties involved (parents, teachers, students, governors, support staff).
- They adopt clear, positive initiatives to promote good behaviour, and invest time and energy in making sure that these are reinforced throughout the school.
- They invest in the motivation of their staff, recognizing and praising the work that is done – not just when it's time for appraisal, but continuously.
- They don't put up smoke screens. In other words, they are honest about what happens in their school and they acknowledge the challenges that teachers have to face. And they *listen* to what their staff have to say.
- They do what they can to provide quality training for teacher and support staff, whether sharing good practice within the school, or paying for trainers.
- They ensure that new staff are given ongoing support and guidance, and, if possible, are protected from commitments or challenges that they do not feel ready for.
- They follow things up, do what they say they will and back

up their staff against unreasonable children or parents.
They NEVER undermine a member of staff in front of a
student.

- They consult with staff before making decisions about
  what should happen to a student that has caused problems,
  i.e. they do not return a student to class before they have
  apologized/made amends with the teacher. They keep
  staff in the 'loop'.
- They run internal exclusions, place students on report or
  withdraw students as necessary.
- They cast a 'don't-mess-with-me' shadow over the students,
  but also have their respect, and are deemed approachable.
- They are available, reliable and *findable* during a crisis!
- They care about the students and put their needs first, but
  not at the expense of their staff's needs. They recognize
  that without a happy staff, the students will suffer anyway.
- They empower staff, allowing them to use their initiative
  and explore new ideas. They demonstrate trust in their
  staff.
- They have strong leadership skills, combining clear vision
  with practical sense.

MANIPULATION

Sometimes you will come across students who are manipulative.
I have certainly met a few. These individuals tend to be bright
and charismatic, and will learn very quickly how to make the
system/situation work for them, perhaps through flattery, lies
or over/under-reacting. They may make subtle little comments,
designed to upset or undermine you. They may act as though
they are impervious to any sanction or consequence – either they
don't take it (or you) very seriously, or they throw a tantrum
about 'unfairness'. They may play their classmates off against each
other, for their own amusement: making sly, provocative remarks
and then passing them off onto someone else … who then gets
blamed. Quite often, these students are social ringleaders, but
equally they can be fairly isolated – their deviousness having
driven others away.

The frustrating thing about these individuals is that, whilst they may be intelligent or have high potential, they are hard to build meaningful relationships with. This makes it difficult for you, as the teacher, to encourage, push, trust or, even, *like* them. I have worked with many students like this, in different schools and different age groups. Many of them have had ESBD, in which manipulative behaviour is just part of many other issues. Often the behaviour has been learned as a coping mechanism, something that has enabled them to deal with difficult personal circumstances, such as battling parents or lack of boundaries, but has become a habit in life.

As the behaviour becomes ingrained, students become over-reliant on it and end up missing one of life's most important lessons: facing responsibility. If you ever work with students like this, make sure you don't allow them to 'play' you. Be honest about how you perceive their behaviour – it is their best chance of getting over it – then bolster their self-esteem with a positive comment:

'Andrew, I know that you are hoping your charming compliments and hard work will get you out of this evening's detention … and you are doing a very good job of acting sincere. But let's face it, *you* know, and I know, that it is just an act. You are a very intelligent individual, and are more than capable of getting through life without having to play games with people.'

MOANING

Moaning students are an inevitable fixture of most classrooms. Maybe it's a whinge about the classroom: too hot, too cold, too noisy, too smelly. Or the level of work: too hard, too easy, too fast, too slow, did it last week. Or sometimes it's that designed-to-be-fun activity that you carefully organized as an afternoon treat: 'What's the point of *this* … it's *boring!*'

Oh, give it a rest, why don't they? Perhaps the key to coping with grumbling students is to not take it too seriously. If you did, you would probably feel like torching the classroom at the end of each day. Humour is often the most effective way of deflecting the moan:

'Whilst I *love* listening to your constant complaining, I'm afraid I have been asked to trial these new sound-blocking ear plugs' (stuff two large pieces of cotton wool in your ears).

or

'I've got an important piece of news for you all. There has been a nationwide ban on anyone using the phrases "do I have to?" or "it's too hot to do work". Anyone caught saying this, or something similar, will have to listen to me singing two verses of Whitney Houston's "I will always love you" after school!'

If you are positive and enthusiastic about your subject this is likely to rub off on your students, helping to decrease the amount of moaning that takes place. Encourage them to be brave, to try things *before* complaining about them. But always keep a look out for the moaning that is justified. Is the classroom really too hot (the chances are you will notice this yourself)? Has the task you've set turned out to be a damp squib? Whilst a bit of humour and encouragement will help your students to lighten up, if real problems are simply dismissed, they will think you don't get it.

MODELLiNG BEHAViOUR

A teacher's job is not just about delivering facts and information – it is about being a role model. Eek! Our students notice what we do, not just in our own classrooms, but all around school (though hopefully not outside of it!). From this they will be learning, interpreting and reflecting on adult behaviour. It is no coincidence that most students will experience some sort of 'crush' on a teacher at some point during their schooling. We are there, guiding and inspiring them, throughout the formation of their understanding of the world.

It stands to reason that if we want to do this amazing (though undeniably scary and demanding) responsibility justice, we need to present a positive example. This isn't about being a pillar of the community or a 'perfect' person. It is about behaving in ways that are reasoned and respectful (at least in front of the students, that is!), whilst still being our own individual selves.

NAME-CALLING

From the ages of approximately eight or nine years to early teens, it is not uncommon for groups of students to get embroiled in the relentless activity of name-calling. If the phrase '*Miss,* she called me a ****!' is a frequent occurrence in your classroom you will know what I mean. Although name-calling can, of course, be cruel and hurtful (see section on 'Bullying'), much of it amounts to petty, attention-seeking behaviour. It is important to know the difference, as name-calling as a form of bullying must be treated very seriously. In its petty form, it can unfortunately cause a lot of time-wasting distraction.

If this is a problem in your lessons, it may be helpful to call a class meeting in which students can be invited to consider the issue, how it interferes with their learning and what can be done about it. If they contribute their own thoughts and suggestions they will be 'part' of the solution. Another option is to invite them to discuss any name-calling problems with you during break-time, in other words, in *their* time, not yours or the lessons'. If anyone pipes up with 'so-and-so said ... ' you can firmly explain that you will happily talk it through at the end of the lesson, but not before. Having to spend time after class may act as a deterrent.

At secondary level, name-calling, 'dissing' or 'cussing' as it is also referred to, can continue to be a significant problem, causing frequent distraction and irritation. As students get older, they tend to find more inventive and cruel ways to wind each other up, and the process can become fraught with tensions about who respects who. It can also lead to aggression and violence – some forms of 'dissing' have a powerful stigma attached to them. To us, as mature adults, this mysterious aura of offence can sometimes seem ridiculous: someone shouts 'Your mum!' and a fight breaks out! What we need to do, however, is endeavour to appreciate that whilst it may not matter to us, such 'dissing' can matter to other generations. It is therefore necessary to treat it seriously and work towards eliminating it from the classroom. Provide opportunities for discussion about why certain words and phrases are hurtful and unacceptable, and emphasize the 'moral' implications of insulting remarks.

NON-VERBAL COMMUNICATION

Much of what we want to say is expressed, not through words, but through our body language. It is important that our physical gestures match and support the ideas that we are trying to convey. This will suggest authenticity (imagine trying to sound forceful and strong, whilst cowering behind a desk and chewing your fingernails!), and will reinforce the message. Effective non-verbal communication includes general considerations such as where you are standing/sitting in relation to your students, and also specific reactions to certain things (raising an eyebrow, or frowning). Here are some suggestions:

- Greet students with a confident smile at the door, which suggests they are welcome but that they are now entering your territory.
- Move around the room during your lessons, so that your presence is felt in different areas of the classroom. Avoid 'pacing' too much when you are talking at the front, as this implies nervousness.
- When addressing the whole class, place yourself in a promi- nent position, preferably at the front where everyone can see you. Sitting behind a desk can convey a sense o

importance and offer a sense of security, but may also be alienating.

- Stand with your shoulders relaxed and feet slightly apart. Lean against something if it helps to 'anchor' you, but be wary of appearing too relaxed.

- Be mindful of your hands. Avoid being 'jittery' or folding your arms (unless you are wanting to be stern). By all means use hand gestures to help express yourself, but make them purposeful and emphatic. Holding a pen or piece of stationery may help.

- Consider your clothing. More business-like dress may mean you are taken more seriously. Casual or 'trendy' clothes will make you more approachable – but anything 'revealing' is a no-no. Comfortable shoes will enable you to move around easily.

- Be congruent – make sure your non-verbal signals match your verbal ones (i.e. your face isn't smiling when your voice is being stern). See section on 'Verbal communication'.

- Smile as much as you can.

- Develop a range of 'looks': surprised, shocked, disappointed, proud, stern, 'I'm waiting …', pleased, perplexed. Sometimes a facial expression is all that is needed.

- When dealing with upset or angry students make sure your body language reflects a sense of calm. Keep hand gestures small, open and close to your own body (no pointing or fist shaking). Allow students personal physical space, and speak in a low, quiet voice.

OBSERVATIONS

An important aspect of effective behaviour management is under-standing the nature of student behaviour. Sometimes a lot can be learned from just watching the way they interact and relate to one another: knowing who sits where in the pecking order, or who doesn't get on with who. These are invaluable pieces of knowledge that can help shape the way we structure our student groupings, making the class easier to manage.

Sometimes we may come across behaviour that is persistently difficult or repetitive, or that may seem completely arbitrary. In this instance, it can be useful to carry out some observations of the student(s) in question, in order to discern what may be triggering the behaviour. Of course, if we are dealing with students with SEN we may be requested to do this anyway, or perhaps allow others to (SENCOs or Educational Psychologists). All behaviour can be explained somewhere down the line, and the closer we can get to these explanations the greater the chance of us resolving it effectively.

Observations are useful with individuals but can also apply to disruptive classes. If we set side aside a few weeks of the term, during which we can invest some energy in monitoring the unfolding events of each lesson, we may start to discover some significant patterns, which can then help to inform our classroom and behaviour management approaches. It may help to consider these questions:

1. What is happening?
2. When do problems occur (break-times, transition times, quiet times, during individual work, etc.)?
3. Where do they occur (standing in line, at the back of the room, in areas of the classroom that are difficult to see)?
4. Are there any obvious triggers (comments from other students, particular tasks, certain students sitting together)?
5. What happens if students are confronted about their behaviour (what interventions do they respond well/badly to)?
6. What brings about change (getting involved with work, distractions, warnings, change of activity, moving students)?

OTHER PUPILS

One of the most frustrating aspects of frequent disruptions is the amount of time and attention that gets sucked away from students who are quietly trying to get on with the lesson. I have had many discussions with teachers and parents about how unfair this is. Unfortunately, in the current climate, there is no simple answer to the problem. Despite efforts made by teachers to multi-task and manage all aspects of the classroom, there are no certainties that behavioural issues will not take up large amounts of time – and that is no reflection on their ability to do their job. It is the nature of the challenging classroom.

Effective behaviour management is a process requiring continuous input and patient attention. Persistent difficulties can rarely be solved with one quick shout – the teacher may have to move students about, soothe hot tempers, chip away at those who refuse to cooperate, chase up missing work, explain things repeatedly, organize sanctions, maintain reward systems and continuously monitor low-level behaviours. As you can see, this does not leave much room for good, old-fashioned teaching!

Perhaps the long-term, long-lasting solution would be to significantly reduce class sizes and improve the student/staff ratio, giving teachers the space to adequately address the learning and behavioural needs of each student, but whether this happens remains to be seen. In the mean time, we have to keep juggling – and using the ideas in this book.

PACE

The pace of a lesson is as important as the content, when it comes to improving behaviour. There is no point in spending 30 minutes recounting an incredibly interesting story to students who get restless after 15. The golden rule is: keep things moving. Plan a series of shorter, related tasks (no more than 20/25 minutes) to fit into a lesson, which could cover different skills or different ways of looking at a problem. For example:

A lesson on persuasive writing (1 hour 10 minutes):

5 minutes	*Starter activity*	Key vocabulary anagrams (on board or whiteboard).
10–15 minutes	*Speaking and listening*	Introduce debate topic. Group discussion: students to move to different sides of room depending on their opinion (agree, disagree, not sure).
10 minutes	*Modelling writing task*	Students to suggest how they would structure a written argument. Model example on whiteboard, using sentence starters to encourage suggestions.

| 20–5 minutes | *Individual work* | Students to produce two paragraphs of persuasive writing based on class debate. |
| 5 minutes | *Plenary* | Share work |

(plus 5–10 minutes flexible time for settling down/packing up/ reorganizing classroom between tasks).

It is important to remember, however, that teaching with pace is not something that can come from a rigid plan. There needs to be enough flexibility to allow for any unexpected changes: sometimes tasks will take less or more time than you predicted, sometimes students will be so absorbed by a piece of work that you would prefer them to continue, sometimes they will be too restless to continue. Be conscious of the mood of the class and be prepared to inject a bit of spontaneity into your practice if necessary. Here are some other suggestions that may help:

- Allow 'thinking' time during question-and-answer sessions (approximately 5 seconds).
- Move around the room.
- When necessary, aim your delivery at students who are chatting, or looking lazy.
- Vary the tone and pace of your delivery: a mixture of fast and slow will keep students on their toes.
- Use a stopwatch or timer to set clear time parameters for activities, which can create a fun, challenging dynamic.
- Break up long chunks of teacher-led discussion by asking questions and giving students 30 seconds to debate their answer with a partner.
- Don't just wait for student attention. Have strategies to help you and the students get started (see section on 'Listening').
- List tasks clearly on the board at the start of the lesson.
- Use a variety of activities: ICT, group work, presentations, etc.
- Focus on skills practised rather than amount of work produced: quality of learning, not quantity.

- Have a backup store of extension activities/worksheets for students who finish early or to maintain momentum.

PARENTS

Effective behaviour management is not just about getting the students on side, but the parents as well. If the worlds of home and school are able to provide a continuum of support with consistent boundaries and expectations, the chances of improved student behaviour will increase. However, this is easier said than done.

All too often, the parents we most need support from are the ones who are least cooperative: those who fail to turn up for meetings, are impossible to track down or behave confrontationally. Is it any wonder that their children are poorly behaved? On the other side, it is important to be sensitive to the fact that some of these parents may have had negative experiences of school themselves. They may regard such establishments with suspicion or mistrust, or may feel insecure about their own lack of academic achievement.

The amount of communication you have with parents will depend on the type of school you work in. In primary schools, contact can be fairly frequent. In secondary schools it is realistic to suppose that you will never meet a large percentage of parents/carers. There is, of course, the obligatory parents' evening/open day, but this can sometimes seem more like a forced ritual than a vital exchange of information. I find it more useful to endeavour to communicate with parents/carers 'as and when'. This way they a) are reassured that I keep close tabs on what's going on with their children, b) know I am approachable should they want to discuss anything and c) don't get the surprise bombshell that their son/daughter misbehaves once a year at parents' evening. I also make sure that I contact parents to tell them about good news as often as possible. Here are some suggestions on how to develop effective lines of communication:

- *Make yourself approachable.* Smile and be warm towards parents. Put them at ease (they may be more nervous than you are). Avoid using teaching jargon.

- *Be diplomatic.* If you are reporting misbehaviour, express sincere regret ('I'm really sorry, but … has been involved in some unacceptable behaviour.') Be serious, but be factual, and use concrete examples of evidence to support what you are saying.
- *Make it clear how parents can contact you if they have questions/ concerns.* Either catching you after school, by phone-call or through appointment. Such an invitation may encourage more wary parents, but will also lay down boundaries for the pushy ones.
- *Remember that a special effort can make a big difference.* Where home/school support is particularly needed, it may be worth establishing a frequent contact system between yourself and the parents/carers (a daily home/school report or notebook, emails, daily text updates). Intense input over a short period of time can have good results.
- *The aim is to provide consistent support.* Discuss ways in which you and the parents/carerscan support one another. For example, establishing agreed targets for the student, developing a home/school reward system, keeping each other informed of difficulties/improvements.
- *Seek support dealing with tricky parents.* If you experience problems, seek advice and assistance from your Head of Year/Department. If a parent threatens you in school or behaves aggressively, explain that you cannot talk to them until they are calm and then seek support from other members of staff. Don't try to take an angry parent on yourself.
- *Keep things simple.* Communicating with parents/carers has the potential to take up a lot of time (especially with those who like to get into lengthy, irrelevant discussions about little Freddy's fishing talents). A postcard or email means you don't have to engage in discussion. However, for important or significant matters, only a phone-call will do.
- *Never give out your personal/home phone-number.* That's asking for trouble!

PHYSICAL AGGRESSION

Despite the media preoccupation with violence in schools, incidents of physical aggression are fairly low down the ranks of regularly occurring disruptive behaviour. Such incidents also tend to be carried out by a small number of students who may have a history of challenging, aggressive behaviour. The problem is perhaps more contained than it is perceived to be – yet this makes it no less worrying or difficult for teachers to cope with. Aggressive behaviour comes in several forms:

- Verbal abuse, threats and menacing language
- Physical provocation: pushing, shoving or gesticulating
- Fighting one-to-one
- Fighting in gangs or groups
- Unprovoked assault
- Attacks involving weapons

At all levels it should be treated seriously, and is definitely one area where there is no room for negotiating or brokering deals ('If I behave for the rest of the lesson, will you let me off my detention?'). It is also an issue that relies heavily on the support between staff across the school, from the senior managers who can withdraw violent students, to the teacher next door, who can help out in an emergency. Strategies for dealing with violent, aggressive behaviour include:

1. *Recognizing early warning signs.* The earlier you can intervene, the greater chance you have of preventing a fight from occurring. Look out for insults, arguments or threatening language, and address these straightaway.
2. *Assessing the risk before wading in.* Don't try to break up a fight or disturbance by yourself if you feel unsafe. The most important thing is to get help. See section on 'Physical intervention' for further information.
3. *Remaining calm, but firm.* Even though your voice may not be enough to break up the fight, you may be able to use it to warn away onlookers. Dispersing the audience often helps.

4.   *Understanding the context of different aggressive behaviours.* Two people fighting is not the same as an unprovoked attack. Hitting out in retaliation or self-defence is not the same as deliberately throwing the first punch.

5.   *Being prepared for a struggle.* If you choose to restrain an aggressive student, you will have to accept the fact that they may struggle, or even lash out at you.

PHYSICAL INTERVENTION

Teachers are given the advice that they may use 'reasonable force' in any situation where a student is at risk of causing harm to themself(selves), to others or to property. It is a rather woolly term, but nevertheless implies that our interventions need to be considered in terms of 'safety' rather than strength. So what constitutes 'reasonable force'? The best answer to this question may be found by going on a physical handling training course, which will not only increase your knowledge and confidence, but will give you 'legal' backup. In general, the considerations you should make when addressing the issue of physical intervention are thus:

1.   *Is it safe to intervene?* If the aggressive student(s) is putting themselves or others at risk, you may feel it is necessary. If, by physically intervening, you are putting yourself at risk, then don't. Seek help. In a fight situation, it invariably requires more than one person to safely separate the brawlers. In big fights, the intervention of whole teams of staff (or even the police) may be needed.

2.   *Can you get help?* Often, one or two students will put themself(selves) forward to get help from other teachers. In some situations, however, students will not cooperate, and it may fall to you to run and find help yourself.

3.   *Are you using minimum force?* If you do decide to intervene, you will need to focus on keeping yourself and the student(s) safe, whilst using minimum force – which is ultimately a very difficult balancing act (hence, the importance of adequate training). Bear in mind that students who are behaving

aggressively may be experiencing surges of adrenalin, and will be extremely difficult to contain with simple arm holds or shoulder grabs – yet further levels of force could be interpreted as assault. Another reason to get other teachers to help: they are witness(es) to what goes on.

POSITIVE RE-ENFORCEMENT

A common feature of classrooms that deal successfully with challenging behaviour is positive atmosphere. From my experience, the most positive atmospheres are often the most stable. Clearly, if students feel welcomed by their teacher, their attitude to the classroom will be less hostile. If the teacher is enthusiastic about creating a vibrant learning environment, and shows commitment to helping students manage their behaviour and remain in the classroom, then the sense of positivity will be reinforced (see section on 'Welcoming environment'). There are many ways to bring positivity into the classroom.

- *Reward systems.* Either whole class or individual. Stickers, stamps, points charts, incentives and prizes. Whatever you choose, keep it simple and keep it meaningful. (See section on 'Reward systems' for more ideas.)
- *Setting targets.* Targets, whether connected with behaviour or learning, can create a goal-focused approach to the classroom, giving students something to aim for and marking achievement. (See section on 'Targets'.)
- *Praise.* The importance of praise cannot be overestimated. Make sure it is purposeful and specific. (See section on 'Praise'.)
- *Creating a welcoming atmosphere.* Make your students feel as though they are welcome and valued in your classroom – including the most difficult ones. Greet them at the door, smile and say that you are looking forward to the lesson. Express enthusiasm for the activities/topics that they will be working on.
- *Positive phrasing.* Express rules, expectations and instructions as positive 'dos' rather than negative 'don'ts'. For example:

'Sit up straight and pull your chair in' rather than 'Stop slouching on your chair'. This takes some practice getting used to, but can become a habit after a time.

- *Give encouragement after a difficulty.* If you have to reprimand a student, offer some kind of optimism at the end of your conversation (e.g. 'I know you can be really sensible at times, so I'm confident that you will go back into the classroom and have a good lesson ...'). Not only will this give a boost to the student's self-esteem, but it will protect your relationship with them – you don't just moan at them, you have faith in them as well.

POWER-SEEKING

Perhaps one of the biggest obstacles to succeeding with managing challenging behaviour is the will of the individual. We cannot, and should not, try to coerce or force our students to do what we want them to, and, sometimes, the more we insist they cooperate, the more they refuse to. This is the inevitable trap of power-seeking behaviour. Imagine this scenario:

Teacher: Stacy, you need to move seats please.

Stacy: Aw, sir! I wanna stay with my mates!

Teacher: Tough! You've spent the whole time chatting to them and you've not done any work. Move over here now please ...

Stacy: No! You can't make me. My mum says I work best when I sit with my mates. You ask her ...

Teacher: Look, I'm not going to argue with you – or your mum. Just move!

Stacy: Tch ... no.

Teacher: Well then, you'll have to leave the room. You can't stay in here if you're not going to do what you're told.

Stacy: You can't chuck me out! I'm staying with my mates.

Teacher: I can and I will!

Stacy: How? I'm not gonna move – and you can't touch me. So what you gonna do?

In this example, the teacher is repeatedly making a rod for his own back by setting up a series of direct, 'no way out' conflicts, and trying to assert his imagined authority over Stacy ('I can and I will!'). She is the strong-willed, argumentative type – would probably argue black was white if she had to. There may not be much genuine rationale to her argument, but once she is backed into a corner she is the kind that doesn't like to lose face – especially when there is an audience of classmates watching her.

Of course, we can feel sympathy for the teacher in this position. His initial request was perfectly reasonable, and his determination to get Stacy to do as she is asked is understandable. He doesn't want the rest of the class to see her getting the better of him – his reputation is on the line. If he gives in, they will think he is weak.

However, in situations like this, the person that 'wins' is usually the one who doesn't care what is lost along the way, the one who is prepared to risk everything. As teachers, we have our professionalism to keep intact, which immediately limits the length to which we can stretch an argument (especially if the use of force is involved). Therefore, by locking into such power-seeking behaviour, we are setting ourselves up to lose. Consider this alternative:

Teacher: Stacy, this is your first warning – if you continue to chat, you will have to move to the front of the class.

(A few minutes pass)

Teacher: Stacy, I'm afraid, as you've continued chatting, I need you to move. There's a seat for you here.

Stacy: Aw, sir! I don't wanna move.

Teacher: Sure, I understand that – but you WERE given a warning. You know the rules of the classroom: one warning then a consequence.

Stacy: I know, but I wanna stay with my mates. Don't make me move sir ... please.

Teacher: You need to move.

Stacy: Sir, please don't make me. I'll be good, I promise.

Teacher: I'm going to help the students who are getting on with their work now. When I come back, I know you will have made the right choice and moved to the front, because I know you wouldn't want the hassle of further sanctions, and I know you are capable of making wise choices. Thank you for cooperating with me Stacy.

The teacher in this instance uses an established system of warning then consequence, and reinforces this by reminding Stacy that it is the agreed rule of the classroom. He also reduces the tension, by empathizing with her ('Sure, I understand'), but makes it clear that she has a responsibility to follow the instruction. He then avoids getting dragged into further argument by simply restating his instruction and eventually moving away from it – he realizes she is 'trying it on'. He phrases his final reminder warmly and positively, as well as giving her the space to move away without the pressure of being watched.

PRAISE

Plenty of praise helps to create a positive, motivating learning environment, and raises self-esteem. It is crucial to improving the attitudes of students with challenging behaviour, who may have experienced very little of it in their lives. However, if it is over-used or dished out without purpose, its good effects can wane. The key is to make praise purposeful, or even tactical:

1. *Make it specific*: 'Well done to the boys in the back row – I can see that the three of you are really focusing on the task ...' If the association between the praise, the particular behaviour and who is doing it is distinct, students will receive clearer messages about what is expected of them.
2. *Give it to students who have 'turned' themselves around*: 'Thank you Lisa, I can see that you've made an effort to be quiet in class today. You've done really well!' Too often, there is so much suspicion surrounding disruptive students that improvements get overlooked. They become trapped in negative expectations. No matter how annoyed you are with a student who caused you problems early in the lesson/week – if they have endeavoured to 'put it right', praise them.
3. *If necessary, be discreet*. Some students find it difficult to deal with praise and positive attention. In fact, I have watched the behaviour of many students start to deteriorate, straight after being praised, perhaps because they have not

wanted to lose their 'rebel' reputation amongst peers. In this instance, do not withhold praise, but make sure you give it discreetly.

4. *Finish on a high*. Spend a few minutes at the end of each lesson, summarizing behaviour and work performance – praise the successes, give positive suggestions for any improvements and highlight the achievements of individuals. 'Well done, 9C! We got a lot of work done today. There was a bit too much noise at times, so tomorrow let's work on keeping our voices down. Apart from that, I think we should be pleased with ourselves. I'd particularly like to say well done to Vicky, Sandeep and Daniel, who managed to complete all of the tasks. And, also, well done to Ricky, who managed to stay in his seat all lesson!'

5. *Use rewards*. Whilst it is arguable that praise itself should be the most powerful reward of all, many teachers have found it helpful to pair praise and success with a reward system of some sort. For ideas, see section on 'Reward systems'.

PREPARATION

We all understand that we need to prepare for learning outcomes by planning lessons and gathering resources, but do we think of preparing for behaviour? Behaviour is often thought of as something that can be difficult to predict, so it always pays to feel ready – preparation gives you a confidence boost and enables you to react calmly and cannily on the spur of the moment. The simplest way to prepare is to clarify in your mind what you do and don't expect in your classroom. This will help you to outline your boundaries to the students, and prompt you to act quickly if they are tested. I have seen many teachers get into difficulties because they simply aren't sure of their own expectations of behaviour, and fail to act consistently. Secondly, it helps to establish a clear framework for how you will deal with any misdemeanours (a system of warnings and sanctions), and how you will reward positive efforts.

Another key way of preparing for behaviour is knowing the students. Ensure that you are familiar with any documentation such as IEPs (Individual Education Plans) and the SEN register. If you are new to a class, talk to other teachers who may have worked with them. Ultimately however, the best way to get to know your students is to a spend time with them. You may then discover that far from being unpredictable, behaviour becomes one of the most predictable things in the classroom!

PREVENTION

Always work to the assumption that prevention is easier and safer than cure. I believe effective behaviour management has three distinct levels:

1.   What is done to *prevent* problems from occurring/developing.
2.   What is done in *reaction* to problems that have already occurred.
3.   What is done to *follow up* after problems have occurred (see section on 'Follow-up')

If enough work is done at the preventative level, the likelihood of needing to do lots of work at the other levels is reduced. Prevention is linked closely to preparation (see previous section), but the other key practices are:

- *Be firm on low-level behaviour.* Firm, consistent attention to little things (calling out, chatting too much, incorrect uniform, eating in class, arriving late (see section on 'Low-level disruption')), will be a deterrent to students who like to do big things, and will establish your reputation as someone who doesn't stand for nonsense.
- *Intervene early.* Don't allow problems to fester or escalate before giving them your attention. For example, a squabble between two children could easily be resolved by some low-level intervention (calming them down, talking through the problem, redirecting them, removing the trigger), but may escalate into a fight if they are left to their own devices – causing you a much bigger headache in the long run.

QUIET

The quest for an appropriate level of classroom noise is down to individual taste. Some teachers prefer students to work in complete silence; some are happy with a bit of background chatter (work related of course!); others like a mixture of both. Personally, I think it should be partly down to teacher expectations, but also partly down to the nature of the students themselves. I have taught in many classes where an expectation of silence was completely futile, caused more trouble than it solved, and certainly didn't provide the key to increased work output. However, I have also taught in classes where a period of silent work helped to focus students and settle the atmosphere. What is right for some may not be right for others.

It is worth remembering that complete silence can be intimidating for shy, withdrawn students, and may draw uncomfortable attention to those asking for help. Too much noise, on the other hand, can be troublesome, making it harder for you to keep track of behaviour and work output, and causing distractions. Here are some suggestions for keeping control of the noise levels:

- *Red/amber/green traffic light system.* Hold up different coloured cards intermittently, as warning or approval of noise levels, or use a pretend volume control (a fake dial backed onto cardboard!).

- *Request 5/10 minute bursts of silence.* Change can help calm the atmosphere down, and can also be used as a bargaining incentive ('too much noise then we will have to work in silence' or 'ten minutes of silent work then we can have a break/earn points').
- *Quiet background music.* Some students respond very positively to the use of music. Keep it quiet and explain that if the music cannot be heard, then the noise level is too high. Again, music has the added advantage of being an incentive.

RECOVERY PLANS

Challenging behaviour is frequently cited as a reason for teachers leaving the profession, and is a major contributor to classroom stress. A significant part of the problem is not the behaviour itself, but how teachers are supported in coping and recovering from it. I have heard numerous horror stories from teachers who have had to just 'carry on' teaching their classes after breaking up severe fights, sometimes in which they themselves have been injured. I, myself, have worked in environments where I have had to leap from one incident to another, with no moment of respite in between.

In contrast, I have also worked in environments where members of staff really support one another – if someone is involved in dealing with a difficult incident, someone else will be there to relieve them from their class, allowing them to take ten minutes to calm down and get a cup of tea. On the surface this may seem fairly trivial, but actually it makes a very important difference. Stress is cumulative. It builds up, one problem on top of another – if an individual feels as though they have no breathing space between challenges, then stress can take over completely. Allowing staff to have a bit of 'recovery time' will help to combat this accumulative effect, keeping them stronger and happier.

Aside from getting a bit of breathing space after a difficulty, there are other things that can be done to help teachers stay emotionally and physically strong when dealing with tough classes (see section on 'Coping'):

- Keep hydrated
- Take proper breaks
- Avoid shouting
- Don't be afraid to ask for support
- Avoid seeking 'perfection'
- Deal with one issue at a time
- Build relaxation into your week
- Know that other people feel the way you do and that other people get ignored/challenged/ridiculed by their students (and it doesn't make them bad teachers)
- Never take things personally.

RELATIONSHIPS

Almost all of what you do to manage classroom behaviour – the strategies you use and the expectations you establish – will be next to useless if you fail to build meaningful relationships with your students. Successful behaviour management relies on cooperative skills: your students are less likely to cooperate with you if they do not respect or trust you; indeed, they may choose to make a point of not co-operating with you. Positive relationships are invaluable.

Of course, not all students make it easy for you to get to know them. Some will go out of their way to alienate themselves – but barriers can be broken down, even with the most hardened of youths! One of the most straightforward ways to do this is through taking an interest in them. Some teachers like to chat about football results or the latest single releases. Personally, I don't like to fake it (I hate football!), so I tend to be frank with them. I explain that I'm interested in getting to know them because I think it will help us to get along. When I ask them what they are into, they usually mutter some variation on 'nothing', drugs or the opposite sex. So I take whatever they say as my starting point – I don't condemn, but simply enquire about what they think makes them interested in drugs/drink/etc. I am often surprised by how intelligent their responses are, by what is revealed when they are talking about things that matter to them. They react positively to the fact that they are being taken seriously on their terms, and from then on in the relationship starts to develop.

One warning: be cautious when building relationships with your students that you do not fall into the flattery trap. Hurrah, they like you! But try not to fear doing things that may potentially disrupt this, such as expecting them to work/telling them off/ enforcing boundaries. In the long term, your relationships will be better protected if you consistently stick by the important boundaries and expectations of the classroom, and prize respect over popularity. Nine times out of ten, students *know* when they have done something wrong, and are expecting to get called up on it – they will not genuinely hold it against you if you do.

REPETITION

Behaviour management does not have to beinventive or 'clever' to be successful. In fact, one of the most effective ways of getting on top of it is to use repetition. Warnings and instructions some-times need to be repeated – if the phrasing is altered, the message can be diluted. If you want to grab attention, raise your voice or vary the tone, but stick to the same script:

'Andrew, you need to sit down.'
'Andrew, you NEED to sit down RIGHT NOW. Thank you.'

As you can see, the language is simple and direct. There is no room for confusion, and the expectation is firmly reinforced the second time. Compare this with:

'Andrew, will you sit down now please.'
'Andrew, I'm tired of waiting. I've told you once … I would like you to stop wasting class time and come and take your seat. Can you hurry up please.'

The second example is not a complete disaster, but a lot of words are wasted in getting the point across. Also, the excess comments add an air of impatience, which implies that the teacher is getting stressed rather than maintaining calm control. Imagine yourself as the student – which version makes you take notice?

Repetition is a useful way of getting key ideas circulating within the classroom. If you use class rules, refer to them frequently. If you want to establish clear expectations, give your students regular reminders. If you need to get a distracted individual's attention, try the 'stuck record' approach: just firmly repeat their name, until they have no choice but to take notice.

REPUTATION

I believe that a reputation can benefit your experience of the classroom – as long as it is a good one! How do you earn a reputation? Establishing it takes time and exposure. In order to make your mark, your students need to see you dealing with problems, handling behavioural issues confidently, being firm, but also maintaining a sense of humour and delivering enjoyable lessons. Fact: children like to talk about their teachers. They are fascinated by us … what we wear, what we eat, where we go and, of course, what we do. And whilst the gossip mill can be vicious, it can also work in our favour: 'I like Miss Farhi. She wears nice clothes, and she always says funny things. Sometimes she's a bit strict, but as long as we're quiet she doesn't mind …' 'Yea … she's alright isn't she?' They tell their friends and siblings, who may, in turn, end up in our classroom one day, and will then tell *their* friends and siblings. And so on.

RESOLUTIONS

If you have dealt with an incident of difficult behaviour, it is likely that at some point soon after, you will have to re-engage with the student and address the problem. Maybe you have agreed to talk to them after class. Maybe you have had to send them out. Or maybe they have had a period of exclusion, and are meeting with you before their return to class. Meetings or discussions such as this are valuable opportunities to repair and strengthen fragile relationships, and to set positive targets for the future.

First things first, you will need to know that the student is calm and ready to have the 'conversation'. If they are still pulling ridiculous faces or yelling with anger, they are not yet in a suitable frame of mind to have a frank and fair discussion (see sections on 'Anger' and 'De-escalation' for ideas on how to deal with wound-up individuals). If they are ready, then approach them calmly, find somewhere quiet and begin the process of making up. The key points you want to address are:

1. Clarification of the facts, preferably in the student's own words. 'Why are we having to have this conversation?'
2. Establishing why their behaviour was unacceptable: 'Why was your behaviour unacceptable?'
3. Establishing a resolution: 'How can you put this right/ make it up to people?'
4. Considering the 'next time': 'What can you do to avoid this happening again?'
5. Making an agreement: 'What are you going to do for the next/rest of the lesson?'

This process will encourage students to recognize that they need to take responsibility for their actions. It is important that the majority of the thinking comes from them, so avoid filling in the gaps yourself. Some teachers prefer to use a written form as the basis for resolution and further discussion (this makes an ideal detention activity). For example:

1. 'I am in detention because ...'
2. 'My decision about my behaviour was poor because ...'
3. 'I can make this up to people by ...'
4. 'In future I can avoid it happening again by ...'
5. 'Next lesson, I will demonstrate this by ...'

Watch out for students with low literacy skills, however, as they may need guidance filling in their answers. End the 'conversation' with some positive reinforcement: remind the student that they are welcome in your lessons, or that although you dislike the behaviour, you enjoy working with them. I realize this can be easier said than done, especially if you have really had your patience tested, but negativity will only compound the problem.

RESOLVING CONFLICT

Having a structured approach to resolving student conflict will make your life easier. If you work within a framework, confusion and stress can be dealt with in a calm, systematic way, and everyone gets to have their say. Otherwise, such situations can easily lead to major argument and physical altercations. Here are some suggestions on setting up a protocol for tackling disputes:

1. *Invite the students to discuss the problem.* Explain that you intend to listen and help them solve the issue fairly. Suggest that the discussion takes place outside the classroom door or away from the 'audience'. (If appropriate, you may wish to ask students to come back after class/during break, but remember that some conflicts are too volatile to be left and will need immediate attention.)

2. *Give each student a 'turn'.* Explain that each individual will get to have their say, so there will be no need for anyone else to interrupt or protest. Once everyone has spoken, concisely reiterate what each person has said, and suggest that it is now time to think about how to move forward.

3. *Discuss thoughts on moving forward.* Go round the party again, asking each person what they think they can do to put the problem right. If you are given silly or antagonistic answers, explain how this will only cause more difficulties – tell them to think again. Praise those who give thoughtful answers.

4. *Enact the resolution agreement.* Get students to apologize/ shake hands/return stolen goods/etc.

5. *Draw your conclusions.* Once everyone has spoken, give your over-arching wisdom on the matter. Confirm that peace has been established, and then praise students for their maturity and honesty.

6. *Keep an eye on the situation.* Unfortunately, no amount of considerate talk will guarantee that the conflict will not resurface. Most classroom arguments tend to be fairly petty, but there are always a few individuals who hold grudges. If you see the words 'I'll get you later!' being mouthed silently across the room, pay close attention.

REWARD SYSTEMS

There are many different and imaginative ways of giving out rewards. The important thing is to find a system that has a motivating effect on your students and is easy to administer. I also favour keeping things streamlined – avoid having several different reward systems going on at once: points for lining up, stars for working quietly, sweets for students who don't chew their pencils, prizes for the busiest tables, golden time for the most hardworking students … it can quickly lead to confusion. One strong points system will usually be satisfactory, and has enough flexibility to cater for both individual efforts and group achievements. It is also general enough to refer to different aspects of classroom life: work, behaviour, specific activities or targets.

You could keep a large chart on the wall, or provide each student with individual ones (although these can be easily lost). It doesn't matter whether you dish out points, ticks, stamps, stars, stickers, etc. – the principle is the same. Used consistently, it provides an effective tool for students of all ages.

The system can be reinforced by the use of prizes or incentives, although this is not always necessary, as some classes seem to get enough fulfilment from the competitive element of who can get the most points. For your toughest classes, however, it is likely that you will need to offer a tangible incentive, something that is concretely motivating, e.g. earn ten points and receive a certificate/record-token/choice of activity. From experience, I would suggest that the most effective incentives are those that can be given 'little and often', and as close in time to the actual achievement as possible. I had enormous success when I set up a system of five to ten minutes 'choosing' time at the end of each morning. Although it took up a bit of lesson time each day, it actually meant that students were much better focused overall. Some alternative suggestions are:

- Writing names on the board of students who make a good start to the lesson, then adding ticks beside their name each time they do something 'good'.
- Handing out raffle tickets for good behaviour (keep and initial the stubs yourself in case students lose theirs).

Have a draw at the end of the week: students earn the
chance to win a prize – the 'luck' element makes it fair
and fun.

- Laminated sheets stuck to tables. Stars/points can be drawn
  on with whiteboard markers. A completed sheet can lead
  to a prize. (Be careful that students don't try to add their
  own points.)

Another point to be considered is that reward systems need to
be fair – they need to take account of the different levels of effort
and ability that exist in the classroom, otherwise they may just
alienate the large number of students that have low self-esteem.
Focus on individual achievement rather than comparisons with
the rest of the class. And think carefully about whether points
can be withdrawn once they have been given – although some
students will respond to such measures, it rather defeats the object
of trying to create something that is positively motivating.

Lastly, do be prepared to change things from time to time.
Reward systems can have a limited lifespan: if the novelty wears
off, so might the benefits. One way to establish whether a reward
system is going to work or not is to develop it with the input
of your students. Ask them what they would be motivated by,
what they think is fair and what deserves reward. There is also
something to be said for the value of good, old-fashioned praise:
nothing will ever replace the importance of sincere, one-to-one,
positive attention.

ROUTINES

Routines help to create a calm, organized environment. With regard
to behaviour, they can provide stability and structure, which will
be reassuring to you and your students (see section on 'Hidden
fears'). Routines can be useful in a number of situations, such as
entering the classroom, tidying up, resolving a difficulty or leaving
the classroom. Once established, they have the added benefit of
allowing students to take a certain amount of responsibility for
themselves – they know what is expected of them, which may
mean you have to nag less.

Your choice of routines will depend on what you want to achieve in your classroom, the nature of your students, your teaching style, your subject and your activities. Therefore I am not going to spell out the specifics, but I will give you some points to consider:

1. *Entering/exiting the room.* Do you want students to enter the room before or after you? Do they stand behind their desks and wait for adult permission, or sit down straight away? Do they line up? Do they enter/leave one by one or as they please?

2. *Organizing equipment.* Are students expected to have certain things out on the desks before the lesson starts (pens, planners, books, etc.), or do you want to keep desks clear from clutter? Are individual students given responsibilities in terms of handing out equipment, or does everyone help themselves? Is frequently used stationery/equipment accessible, and are students trusted to get it when they need it, or do they need to ask for permission? Are students familiar with health and safety procedures?

3. *Tidying up.* Does a certain amount of time need to be allocated to tidying up or can it be done at the last minute? Do students have specific jobs and responsibilities? Do they know where to put equipment or unfinished work? Do you need to 'count in' returned items?

4. *Homework.* Is it set at the start or end of the lesson? Is it written up on the board or do you explain it verbally? Do students have a specific place to record the task? Is the handing in date clear? Do you collect it at the start/end of the lesson? Do you have a procedure for dealing with late or missing homework?

5. *Dealing with 'upsets'.* Is there a place in (or out of) the classroom where wound-up students can calm down? Are students given a set number of warnings before being given a sanction?

RUDENESS

I don't recall reading a section on 'putting up with personal comments and insults' in my job description, but it has, at times, been a rather common feature of my working day. From the subtle, 'Miss, when are you leaving?' to the brazen, 'I hate you, you cow!' – I have heard language more colourful than I ever knew existed. Over the years I have learned that crude remarks thrown at me by a bunch of moody teenagers have absolutely no impact on the quality of my life. In fact, they say more about the lives of the teenagers, than about me. But it wasn't always like that – when I first began teaching, I was not too far in age from some of my students, and keen to make a good impression. The occasional bit of adolescent cheek would leave me reeling.

Some teachers would argue that this profession is not for the faint-hearted, that students will pick on any hint of insecurity and then play on it: appearance, personality, teaching style, mannerisms. If the response to these things is emotional, then of course they will hurt. One of the most common side effects is loss of confidence, which, in turn, makes it harder to deal with further comments and behaviours. The situation is particularly tough for new teachers and trainees, who may not have the range of strategies and experience to effectively handle difficult classes, but may also find that their emotions are the dominant force in how they react – the thick skin takes a while to grow.

Of course, the key is not to take things personally. Sometimes it helps just to remind yourself that, no matter how bad your students try to make you feel, your life is still a million times better than theirs. Other approaches include:

- *Emphasizing respect.* Rather than demonstrating personal offence, relate student rudeness to the expectations of respect. Respect is something that seems to matter a great deal to young people. 'We have very clear rules about being respectful in this classroom – think carefully about what you are about to say …'
- *Keep calm.* Use a businesslike, neutral tone of voice. 'I don't want to hear it.' Avoid raising your voice or getting worked

up – if you become flustered, your students may play on this in subsequent lessons.

- *Keep cool.* Make it clear that you are not embarrassed, but impress upon your students that rudeness is unacceptable. It can be helpful to address the issue privately/after class with some words along the lines of, 'Do you think it's fair that teachers in this school have to deal with unpleasant remarks?'

- *Use empathy.* Relate personal comments and insults to students' own experiences: 'How would you feel if I said … to you?'

- *Use humour.* One way to show your students that their insults are not going to work is to make them seem ridiculous – a huge bout of fake crying will do the trick, as will agreeing with them: 'Sir, you look like a tramp!' 'Thank you but I think that's an insult to tramps!'

- *Take racist/sexist remarks seriously.* Your school should have a clear policy for dealing with this problem. Inform students that because of the unacceptable nature of their comments, you will have to follow school procedures in dealing with the matter.

SEATING PLANS

If you take control of student seating arrangements, you may find that your classroom becomes a much easier place to manage. Control means that *you* decide who sits where, or at least, have the right to move students about if they are being disruptive. This is something that is best communicated to the class at the start of the year/term. I favour a flexible approach that encourages students to take responsibility for their own actions and opportunities:

1. Students sit where I tell them to initially. If I don't know the class, I allocate them seats alphabetically or boy/girl. I inform them that they will eventually have the opportunity to choose their own seats, once I have seen that they can be sensible.

2. If the current arrangement causes problems, I make adjustments until it starts to work, frequently reminding them that after a period of settled classroom life, they will *earn* the chance to choose their seats.

3. All being well, I give them the opportunity to choose, but under clear agreement that, should there be any problems, I get to make my own adjustments.

4. If things get out of hand, the seating plan returns to my complete control. If not, then students continue to choose.

This system has worked very well for me, as it allows me to hold a tight reign on the overall space, whilst still investing trust and responsibility in my students. It is also important to consider that it is not just where *students* are seated, but how desks are arranged, that will affect your lessons. Groups? Clusters? Pairs? Singles? Rows? Horseshoes? In many classrooms the flexibility of seating arrangements will be restricted by the size, shape and nature of room use, but if you can, experiment – different formations can create very different atmospheres.

SELF-CONTROL

My experience has taught me that students with behavioural difficulties frequently fall into two categories: those who can't help losing control, and those who can't bear losing it. The former relates to students who get carried away with themselves, or feel compelled to act up in front of their classmates, and also includes those with particular disorders such as AD(H)D – the type that can do little more than shrug and nod when you question them over their choice of action. The latter refers to students who will do anything to retain their own sense of 'power' – those who refuse to cooperate, who will argue back, intimidate or try to undermine you.

In both instances, a stable, structured environment with clearly enforced boundaries and expectations can help to keep things running smoothly. What I have also noticed is that the 'loses control' type of student often responds well to a very firm, no-nonsense approach, whereas the 'wants to keep control' student will be more likely to come round to reasoning and negotiation (if they perceive that they are being 'bossed' about, they may become confrontational). I'm not suggesting that we should wildly vary our discipline styles depending on the nature of our students (consistency is, after all, one of the golden rules), but that it is always useful to be sensitive to these issues and to recognize that the manner in which we approach our students can effect the outcome.

SELF-ESTEEM

Issues of self-esteem are often cited in relation to behavioural problems. Low self-esteem is the common culprit, but it has also been suggested that some challenging behaviour is the result of very high levels of self-esteem: too high in fact – the students who always think they are right, or think that they have the right to do as they please. Personally I believe that even the arrogant, cocky, over-confident students may be unwittingly employing this bravado to conceal some deep-rooted insecurities about themselves. Other students will wear their esteem on their sleeves: the ones who are easily upset, or frequently complain that they 'can't do it'. Some will seem to lack aspiration and motivation. They may come across as lazy or disengaged: what's the point in trying when you're worth nothing and going nowhere? It is a vicious cycle.

Of course, the development of positive esteem begins with a stable, nurturing home-life, which not all children get to experience. However, as teachers, there are measures we can take to encourage the esteem of young people within the school environment, which will, in turn, benefit the rest of their lives:

- Give frequent praise and make it meaningful (see section on 'Praise').
- Notice improvements as much as achievements.
- Take an interest in them (see section on 'Relationships').
- Use a reward system that addresses *individual* achievements and contributions (see section on 'Reward systems').
- Set achievable targets, and give lots of encouragement (see section on 'Targets').
- Never make personal remarks or criticisms, even if students do it to you.
- If students are shy or withdrawn avoid putting them on the spot or singling them out in front of the class.
- Make it clear that everyone has different strengths and weaknesses, and that people work at different rates and have different skills.
- Encourage students to engage in activities or clubs that they enjoy and will raise their confidence, e.g. sports, music, drama, art.

- Try to engage students in conversations about their opportunities and future aspirations.
- Remind students of their previous successes and express your faith in them.
- Be rigorous. Don't allow students to 'slip away' – make them accountable for their work, behaviour and attitude. Explain that you won't make exceptions for them, because you want them to do it and *know* that they can.

SEN

A proportion of students exhibiting challenging behaviour have a statement of special educational needs and BESD, which recognizes their difficulties in an official capacity and may lead to additional support and resources. If you work with students with BESD, it is important to understand what their individual needs are, and to take these into account when you are considering their behaviour. Here is an overview of the types of SEN you may encounter, although the most useful source of information is usually the SEN staff at your school:

- *AD(H)D (Attention Deficit (Hyperactivity) Disorders)*. Core behaviours associated with AD(H)D are hyperactive/impulsive behaviour (restlessness, fidgeting, poor self-control, acting 'silly', demanding, acting without thinking, low frustration tolerance) and inattentiveness (poor concentration, easily distracted, forgetful, disorganized).
- *ODD (Oppositional Defiant Disorder)*. The student who is 'in your face' and will commonly refuse to cooperate, say 'no' on principle and argue persistently.
- *CD (Conduct Disorder)*. Behaviours can include lying, cheating, stealing, threatening and cruelty.
- *OCD (Obsessive Compulsive Disorder)*. Individuals will have fixations and ritualistic behaviours.
- *SLD (Specific Learning Disabilities)*. Dyslexia, Dyspraxia or Dyscalculia, language and communication disorders, which may lead to secondary behavioural problems, as a result of frustration and low self-esteem.

- *Depression/Anxiety.* Depressed individuals will become moody, sad, withdrawn and/or preoccupied. They may also become more irritable.
- *ASD (Autistic Spectrum Disorders).* Individuals have difficulties forming social relationships, communication, creative play and limitations on imagination. They may exhibit aggressive behaviours.

When dealing with SEN, the first principle is to get to know the individual and to endeavour to understand their particular needs and issues. Establish as much routine and structure into your lessons as you can, and have a fair, prearranged system of rewards and consequences. Focus on positives and esteem-building praise as much as possible, and always look at the context of the behaviour (Could they help it? Were they provoked?), but don't allow students to make excuses – encourage them to be responsible for their actions. Always avoid escalating a situation by being confrontational, over-harsh or personally critical.

Oh ... and don't assume that every student who exhibits difficult behaviour requires a statement of SEN – some of them *are* just naughty for naughty's sake!

SEXUAL BEHAVIOUR

Inappropriate sexual behaviour is perhaps more common than we would wish it to be. It ranges from flirtatious games of 'footsie' under the classroom table to serious sexual harassment. If it happens in our classrooms, it is helpful to have an idea of how we will deal with it, as this will alleviate the potential awkwardness and embarrassment that such behaviour may cause.

Avoid drawing attention to the behaviour and don't try to humiliate the students involved. Sexual behaviour happens for a number of reasons, but blatant activity within the public space of the classroom can often relate to students being 'needy': the ones who seek reaction and approval from their peer groups, or want to get attention. Discreetly inform them that you want the behaviour to stop and that you will need to speak to them after class. If it can't wait, invite them to discuss it with you outside the room. Be prepared for the fact that their actions may be intended to provoke or humiliate you. Speak to them in a calm, firm manner, and if they test you, explain:

'I simply don't want that behaviour in my classroom, so it needs to stop. I'm not embarrassed by it – my concern is that it is inappropriate and against school policy and I may have to inform your Head of Year, and also your parents, which could be very embarrassing for you.'

Treat it seriously but don't overreact, as this may be the response they hoped to get from you. If the behaviour fizzles out after you have spoken to them, a discreet word with their tutor/Head of Year will do. If the behaviour persists, or is more serious in nature, then a formal discussion will need to be had, and your CPO (child protection officer) may need to be informed.

SHOUTING

Shouting at your students is always best avoided. It damages your voice, increases your stress levels, creates tension and stress in the classroom, and is, more often than not, ineffective. It can also suggest to your students that you are losing control of a situation. So what are the alternatives? And is it okay to shout occasionally? The voice is one of your main professional tools. It can be applied in a variety of ways, but also needs to be looked after.

In preference to shouting, effective teachers often develop a firm, deep tone of voice that is adopted whenever class/student attention is needed. This is not a level that is maintained throughout the lesson, but is used tactically. The rest of the time they may speak at a lower volume and in a 'friendly' manner. They will also have good projection, and are able to send their voice to all corners of the room, without straining.

Occasionally, a situation may arise, such as a fight, in which the need to distract and quickly get attention is required. The natural temptation is to shout, and if you rarely shout at other times, it may do the trick. However, if students are completely absorbed in their own antics, no amount of shouting will distract them and your efforts may be wasted. Perhaps one of the most effective ways of getting student attention, assuming it is safe to do so, is by approaching them personally – moving towards them and talking in the normal, respectful tones that you would use when talking to any other adult. This is non-confrontational, respectful and calm.

STEALiNG

For some schools, petty theft is a daily occurrence. I have spoken to many teachers who feel they have to lock everything away or keep close count of every piece of equipment they lend out. They are unable to turn their backs for a second. It seems that the science and technology departments suffer the greatest losses: test tubes, safety goggles, glue-guns, nails … but any classroom is vulnerable. The desired swag ranges from little items such as pens and Blu-tack, to the more serious mobile phone/wallet category. The students steal from the classroom, they steal from home, they steal from each other, or they steal from you. It's pretty sad really.

And of course, the result is the aforementioned sense that everything needs to be nailed down or checked in, which wastes valuable time and creates a climate of suspicion. The most inspired solution I have come across regarding the safeguard of loaned stationery is the 'I give you something, you give me something' principle. If students cannot bring or borrow their own pen/pencil (see section on 'Lack of equipment'), they can borrow one from the teacher, *only* if they hand over something of theirs (a watch/mobile phone/*shoe*) as deposit. Teachers who have used this system claim they have never had problems getting stuff back. Other strategies include:

- Spot checks.
- Having a 'friendly' 'Please check your bags and pockets before leaving the room' notice on the door, and apply it consistently for a few weeks – don't make a big thing of it, just take back the equipment that 'mysteriously' found its way into their bags.
- Asking students how they would feel if stuff was taken from them or from members of their family.
- If you can find it, showing students some video/documentary footage of schooling in poverty-stricken countries, where children sometimes miss out on education because

they cannot afford pens and books – this usually makes an impact.

- Stationery vending machines or discount school shops.

Theft of valuable personal items should be treated seriously. Management will need to be informed immediately. Hopefully they will be supportive, but if you have concerns contact your union. Parents, and possibly the police, will need to be notified. It is important, however, that you yourself take reasonable measures to protect your things: don't flash them about and don't leave them visible and unattended. Avoid creating opportunities for those who find it difficult to avoid helping themselves.

SWEARING

Swearing is a funny one. We all allow those four-letter words to slip from our mouths occasionally, yet convention suggests we do not tolerate them in the classroom. The confusion is only compounded when we hear little Freddy innocently explaining: '… but my mummy says it all the time!' Children and young people have a natural inclination to explore and experiment with language. They may seek to test the effect of certain words or phrases, and the majority of this is harmless and normal. However, if a class is allowed to get away with swearing, there is a risk that they will then feel their 'relaxed' teacher won't mind if they turn up late/chat to their friends/avoid work – treacherous ground!

The words themselves are empty – they are *just* words. It is the meaning we attach to them, the ideas they represent, that cause trouble. Swearing = rude, vulgar, insulting language. Swearing = loosening of moral standards. Swearing = breakdown in society. Swearing = out of control. And loss of control, as any teacher knows, is bad for the classroom. In order to maintain control, we need to demonstrate that there are boundaries of acceptable/ unacceptable behaviour, and the use of language is a straightforward way of doing this.

Stamping swearing out completely is unrealistic, but having clear expectation that it is unwanted in the classroom will help. I always relate swearing or inappropriate language to the rule of respect, but I avoid blowing it out of proportion:

'Please be careful with your language. We have a rule about respect in this classroom, and I wouldn't want you to get into trouble for breaking that rule. That's your first warning.'

If you discuss ground rules at the start of the year, inevitably the issues of swearing and respect will come up – a useful starting point for encouraging students to take ownership of their actions in the classroom. Help them to decide that swearing and foul language is disrespectful and therefore unwelcome. As with all behaviours, if you are tenacious and consistent in dealing with it, students will get the message and the problem will decrease.

It is also worth considering the context of swearing. Accidentally cursing as a pot of water spills all over your beautiful artwork, is different from swearing at a classmate who has called you 'big nose' for the fifth time that day, which is also different from hurling unprovoked swear words at someone just to wind them up.

IS FOR...

TAKE-UP TIME

Appropriate student responses to our commands and requests do not always happen as quickly as we would like them to – this does not mean they will not happen at all. One of the fatal mistakes teachers often make is losing patience too quickly: giving a first warning and then a second and third warning immediately after, or bypassing the warnings altogether and going straight for the ultimatum. Understandably, teachers do not want to waste time waiting for one individual to respond, at the expense of attending to the rest of the class, but being too hasty can have unfortunate consequences – students will often become argumentative and confrontational if they feel they are not being given a 'fair chance'.

Take-up time gives students the space and time to make positive decisions about their behaviour, and to follow instructions or requests without the pressure of someone looking over their shoulder. If you give a student a warning, make sure they have heard and understood it, and then move away from the situation – have a conversation with some other students or carry on talking to the whole class. Refocus your attention on the misbehaving student a minute or two later. If they have responded appropriately to your warning, then acknowledge this with a discreet nod or thank you. If they are continuing to behave inappropriately, give a second warning or consequence. The time-lapse in between warnings is important because it allows attention to be drawn away from the offending student.

TARGETS

Targets can be useful in a number of ways. They are a helpful means of motivating students academically and therefore raising achievement, and can be used to break down learning objectives into manageable chunks. They can also be used in relation to behaviour, either for the whole class, small groups or individuals. They can be changed daily, weekly or even termly, and can relate to specific problems (chatting, calling out, getting out of seats, arguing, answering back, etc.) or times (lining up, getting ready for activities, tidying up, etc.). They can also build upon previous achievements. For example:

'Our target for this week is to get ourselves ready and lined up for PE in seven minutes. Remember last week, how we managed to do it in under ten minutes – I bet we can improve on that!'

The benefit of whole-class targets such as this is that they create a unifying challenge for the class – getting ready on time becomes something fun and positive. Success can be rewarded, creating opportunity for praise and improved self-esteem. The downside of whole-class targets is that some students may become alienated if they end up letting the side down, and there will always be those few who try to antagonize the class by refusing to cooperate.

It may be necessary to differentiate targets within the classroom, so that they are meaningful to students with different needs and challenges, in which case, individual targets can be more effective. Students with specific behavioural difficulties may really benefit from personalized support in this way. In general, useful targets need to be:

1.   *Meaningful:* students need to be made aware of them, and be interested in achieving them, so agree on them together.
2.   *Achievable:* break long-term aims down into smaller steps, so they that the student can experience success, and recognize 'milestones' of improvement.
3.   *Specific:* make them clear, simple and succinct and avoid

generalized phrases such as 'improve behaviour'. Use language that the students can understand.

4.   *Measurable:* both you and the students need to be able to identify when a target has been reached. It can be helpful to include criteria for this within the target ('To line up quietly every day for a week').

5.   *Time-restricted:* if targets are allowed to carry on indefinitely, they lose their impact, so review them frequently, and keep reminding students of their goals.

TEACHING ASSISTANTS

Teaching assistants can make an invaluable contribution to the management of classroom behaviour. They are an extra pair of hands, eyes, ears and mouth and are potentially one of the best resources a teacher can have. Teamwork is the key, however, a successful working relationship may not automatically fall into place. It may be something that needs to be established, or that needs to be continuously nurtured. Here are some tips:

•   Be honest but diplomatic. Too much criticism is demotivating; lack of honest feedback can lull people into a false sense of security.
•   Focus on supporting one another, and building team spirit: talk about 'we' rather than 'you' and 'I'.
•   Make staff feel valued by asking for their advice/opinion/ ideas. Recognize that they may know more about some students than you – value their knowledge.
•   Assign clear, specific roles, to avoid confusion and overlap. Try to utilize individual strengths (e.g. artistic skills, caring nature, sense of humour, organizational skills, multi-tasking).
•   Arrange frequent opportunities to evaluate progress at the end/start of the day. Pre-arrange these where possible to make it easier for staff.
•   Encourage and support staff in finding quality training in behaviour management.
•   Make sure you have a clear behaviour policy of your own. If you don't know what you want, how will anyone else?

- Try to turn differing classroom 'styles' into strengths (e.g. good cop/bad cop, strict/gentle) – contrasts can work as long as you are on the same team.
- Be appreciative.

TEAMWORK

Schools that experience success when dealing with challenging behaviour almost certainly have a staff that work together and cooperate as a 'united front'. Teamwork is vitally important, both in terms of departments/year groups, and the wider school environment. It is vitally important, but it can also be hard to maintain. Unfortunately, I hear frequent stories about staff members failing to support each other, either through bullying, undermining or not pulling their weight. Some schools suffer from a lack of stability, with high turnovers of staff and constant change. It is a frustrating and potentially damaging situation to be in, but on the positive side, nothing is permanent. Atmospheres within schools can and do change: new leadership, restructuring, improved buildings, new faces ... and if all else fails, there is always that other school down the road.

The key ways in which staff can help each other to effectively manage behaviour are:

1. *Sharing information.* Concerns about student welfare, rumours of emerging disputes or outbursts, recent incidents, staff/timetable/room changes – these are all useful bits of information to know and pass on, and will help staff to plan ahead and prepare effectively.
2. *Sharing responsibilities.* If you coordinate with other staff, you may be able to save yourself a lot of time and effort, for example, taking turns to run department detentions, or having a 'cooling off' system where disruptive students can be 'looked after' in other classrooms. This can work well as long as the burden is evenly spread.
3. *Active support.* It is a great relief to know that, should you face dealing with a fight or aggressive student behaviour, help is at close-hand. For physical intervention (see section

on 'Physical intervention') it is essential that you don't go
it alone. However, there may need to be agreed protocols,
so that staff know exactly how and when to intervene
– sometimes another person's input can cause more
problems than it solves.

4.   *Moral support.* That disastrous PE lesson doesn't seem quite
so awful when you are laughing about it with your colleagues at break. Staff camaraderie is invaluable. It enables
us to lighten up and reminds us that we are not alone.
Good relationships within the staffroom are the glue that
keeps some teachers working in very tough schools.

TiME-OUT

Offering students space and time to remove themselves from a
problematic situation, in order to calm down and reflect, can be a
very effective way of managing difficult outbursts. It encourages
students to take responsibility for their own aggression, excitement
or upset, and to develop vital *self*-management skills. For nervous
or easily wound-up students, it provides an opportunity to
temporarily get away from stressful situations. For show-offs, it
shields them from that all-important audience. And in volatile
situations, it allows us to get students away from one another, or
from the things that are triggering their problematic behaviour.

The majority of teachers I have come across use time-out in
one form or another. They may not always call it 'time-out' and
may not adopt it in the systematic way that some primary and
special schools do, but there is clearly a recognized common-
sense in giving troubled individuals a bit of breathing space,
rather than trying to brow-beat them into cooperating.

Personally, I believe that the most effective use of time-out
relies on it being part of the classroom routine – an established
and recognized approach to difficult behaviour that both staff and
students commonly understand. If it is only used occasionally,
or arbitrarily, its potential to create a calm and stable classroom
environment is diminished. Once students are used to it, and if it is
applied consistently, it can have enormous benefits. It is a powerful
preventative measure (see section on 'Prevention'), enabling the
teacher to curb and diffuse problems at the earliest opportunity:

'Russell, I can see that you are getting a bit over-excited over there – I'd like you to take a 2-minute time-out, thank you. When you are calmer, you can go straight back to the art table and carry on.'

It is important that time-out is not viewed as a punishment but as an opportunity to sort oneself out in a positive way – it is often referred to as 'turn-around time'. It can also be self-administered, which reinforces its self-management properties. Some points to consider:

- *Do students understand how it works?* The process and its benefits will need to be clearly communicated to students, in order that they do not assume it is negative. Explain that it is a positive opportunity to calm down and put things right, *instead* of receiving a consequence or sanction (see section on 'Choice').
- *How long should it be?* Time-out should be brief (no more than 5 minutes, unless in extreme circumstances) – it is NOT the same as removing a student who is causing problems. It can be helpful to provide a timer (plastic sand timers are a useful visual cue, or stopwatches). Brevity also discourages students who hope to use it to avoid work.
- *Where should it be?* In an ideal world, there would be a small, private space attached to the classroom. If not, then a specific chair or area of the room can be used – as long as it is relatively distraction free. Alternatively, a chair may be placed outside the classroom door (although some schools are against this as it can create additional problems).
- *Is there a protocol?* After a time-out, students should be expected to 'check-in' with you before returning to the group – this can be as simple as a nod, or otherwise, a quick 'chat' just to check that they are suitably calm, and if necessary, apologetic. Other class members should be reminded that students on time-out are not to be talked to or wound up further.
- *Are the positives reinforced?* I always make a point of praising students who use time-out appropriately and remind them that it is a mature way of dealing with a difficulty.

- *What if students self-administer?* You may wish to develop some sort of code for students who choose to take themselves on time-out, which will avoid confusion. A discreet gesture or a laminated time-out request card can be effective.

TRIGGERS

Anticipating and understanding behavioural triggers can be invaluable to your classroom management practice. Think of a trigger as anything that 'sets off' a pattern of problematic behaviour. Common examples include:

- Comments made by other students (insults and jibes or anything involving people's 'mums'!)
- Interaction between certain individuals (those that don't get along or get along too well)
- Bullying
- Grudges and historical difficulties between students, or even their families
- Particular tasks
- Certain teacher approaches (too strict, too soft, too aggressive)
- Perceived unfairness or victimization
- Classroom environment (too hot, too cold or too noisy, awkward room arrangements and 'open' spaces)
- Fear of failure and insecurities about academic ability (level of work is too hard, or is perceived to be too hard)
- Boredom (level of work is too easy, or lacks appeal)
- Change (of teacher, room or activity)
- Unsettling weather
- Incidents around school (e.g. fights or particular events).

If you are aware of these things as they arise, you can intervene at an early stage and therefore minimize the chance of further problems unfolding, or at least prepare yourself for the after-effects. As has been stated previously, once you have got to know your students and their triggers, challenging behaviour has a rather predictable nature, as opposed to the unpredictable one it is often perceived to have.

It is possible that some students will react to things that others wouldn't. I knew a number of students who used to fly off the handle about seemingly trivial things: blunt pencils, people leaving the door open, particular sandwich fillings. Understanding these quirks is all part of getting to know your individual students, and may require some sensitivity on your part.

There may also be situations where poor behaviour is difficult to make any sense of at all. If so, spend some time monitoring the activity within the classroom (see section on 'Observations'), and take time to reflect on what you see – things often come to light when you step back from them. If you find it hard to be objective, you may wish to invite a trusted colleague to observe a typical lesson – as an outsider, they can identify triggers that you have been unable to spot.

TRUANCY

Poor attendance is a major issue for many schools and often goes hand-in-hand with poor behaviour. Unfortunately, it can become a vicious cycle. Difficulties coping with the rigours and expectations of school are a deterrent to going in. Once you stop going in regularly, the rigours and expectations become even harder to cope with. Some students spend days and weeks at a time not where they are supposed to be, and at worst, their parents condone this or do nothing about it. The situation also creates relentless problems for teachers, who have to chase up coursework from perpetually absent students, or suddenly have to accommodate those who have missed most of the term's work.

Another issue is the students who are known to be in school, but are not appearing in the right places at the right time. Where are they? Smoking behind the terrapin huts or lurking in the toilets, no doubt. Students who 'bunk off' are the bane of senior management life, for not only are they missing lessons, but there is also a strong possibility that they are causing disruption in and around the building.

Dealing with poor attendance is a whole-school, and even whole-community, issue. To a certain extent, as a humble teacher, you will be at the mercy of how effectively your school deals with it. There are a few things you can do, however, to improve or safeguard attendance of your own lessons:

- *Good attendance rewards.* Points, stickers, stars and certificates for those who attend regularly and on-time. Some may sneer at the idea of rewarding students just for turning up, but if it at least gets them through the door …
- *A clear policy for dealing with unexcused lateness.* Short detentions to make up time missed, preferably on the same day.
- *Phone-calls home for repeat offenders.* This can have a big impact, but depends on the attitude of the parents – although it may be worth reminding them that they have a legal responsibility to address their child's attendance, and could be referred to an Education Welfare Officer.
- *Going on 'report'.* This strategy can be effective for those who want to please and improve, but are otherwise easily led. It has the benefit of being monitored by every teacher in every lesson.
- *Strong words.* Some students respond well to a reality check, 'If you keep missing school, your grades *will* suffer – as someone with lots of potential, you owe it to yourself … etc'. Showing a student that you care about them being there can make a difference.

IS FOR ...

UNDERLYING REASONS

The issue of awareness has already been discussed (see section on 'Awareness'), but I wish to restate its importance. All behaviour has a reason – not an *excuse*, but a reason behind it. If we do what we can to understand the reason(s), we are in a much better position to take the right course of action and to address the problem meaningfully. Behaviour is a good indicator of mood, and because of the unique involvement a teacher has with their students, they are sometimes the first to notice if something is up. A child starts having uncharacteristic temper-tantrums, or suddenly becomes quiet and withdrawn. Perhaps a previously hard-working student loses motivation and drops out of lessons, or a socially popular individual becomes isolated and argumentative. All young people experience their ups and downs – it is part of the growing-up process – but sometimes it may be clear that significant issues are afoot. Not everyone is willing or confident enough to talk about their problems, so keeping a thoughtful eye on behaviour enables us to be vigilant.

A student I used to work with would have Jekyll and Hyde type changes of behaviour depending on which parent they had stayed with over the weekend. It transpired that one of the parents would spoil them, and the other would thump them. Obviously, not all behaviours or causes are that extreme. Sometimes underlying problems may seem insignificant or trivial, however they may still have a powerful impact on a child's attitude and behaviour in school. I am often told stories about teachers having difficulties with high-achieving, middle-class students – those who come from 'good' backgrounds, and who, in theory, have everything going for them. The scenarios I hear most often are about highly-strung, stroppy little madams and arrogant, lazy, cocksure young men who believe it is the teacher's job to secure them the best exam grades.

Without wishing to generalize or make assumptions, I can't help thinking that having a 'privileged life' does not necessarily equate to having a stable, happy, emotionally sound background. Coupled with the stories of attitude problems and difficult behaviour, often come stories of parents who work long hours and are rarely present, or provide inconsistent parenting models, or who over-indulge their children materialistically and/or emotionally.

UNSTRUCTURED TIMES

The likelihood of problematic behaviour occurring often increases during unstructured times, such as break and lunchtimes, free-play, transition between lessons and, even, between tasks. The change of focus and relative freedom seems to create an excited energy, which can easily lead to trouble. Of course, there is a definite need to allow students space and time to 'let off steam' – too much order and rigidity can be equally damaging, so sometimes it has to be a balancing act.

If your school has a clear code of conduct that is consistently reinforced, unstructured times will be less hazardous – most students will be aware of expectations, and will be more responsive should staff need to remind them of their limits. It comes down to control, and in a sense, creating 'structured unstructure': for example, corridors that are regularly monitored, well-organized playground areas and activities, clear procedures for moving around the building.

Within your own classroom, routines are essential (see section on 'Routines'). Teachers who don't use them and who frequently deliver unstructured, disorganized lessons are likely to suffer the consequences. Routines become particularly useful during those transitional moments, when students are arriving, leaving, moving around the room, or getting equipment out/putting it away. Here are some guidelines:

- *Make sure students wait for the cue*: give them the instructions, check that they understand, *pause* and then ask them to get underway. Pausing will allow you to establish a sense of calm.
- *Give clear, simple instructions:* use uncluttered phrases and straightforward language (this may require some practice – it isn't as easy as it sounds) and if necessary write the phrases on the board. For frequently used routines try a simple repeated prompt, for example: 'Coats. Books. Bags.'
- *Stagger the movement:* if the students are moving to another area, instruct them to do so table-by-table, enabling you to monitor their behaviour and maintain a sense of order, as well as avoiding a mass rush.
- *Give responsibility to students:* individuals can be asked to hand out equipment or exercise books, minimizing the need for large groups of students to be getting it themselves. Generally, students like to have responsibility and will enjoy the privilege.
- *Set specific time limits:* using a stopwatch or timer can be very motivating, and provides clear boundaries, minimizing time-wasting.
- *Emphasize health and safety:* this is particularly important during practical sessions or where extra precautions need to be taken.
- *Minimize unnecessary movement:* have a classroom policy on when and how students can move about the room. Do they have to have a particular purpose? Do they need to ask for permission? Is there a particular route they should take?
- *Prepare students for change:* let students know how much time they have left on a particular activity or what will be happening next: 'In a moment we will be rearranging the desks for our drama session ...'
- *Create areas:* this is particularly useful in the primary class-room, where several different activities may be going on

at once (e.g. art and crafts, ICT, quiet reading, dressing up, topic work, science and discovery). The appropriate equipment can be stored in these areas, minimizing the need for stuff to be spread all over the classroom – particularly useful for messy activities!

- *Organize activities and resources in advance:* where this is possible, it can make an enormous difference to the management of transition times within your classroom – if things are ready, you will have less need to 'flap', and this will have a stabilising influence on your students. It is also worth having a stash of emergency or extension activities to occupy those who complete tasks quickly.

UNUSUAL NOISES

It is highly likely that, at some point during your teaching career, you will encounter that group of students who think it is amusing to antagonize you with silly noises: some sort of hum or whistle, that is loud enough to be distracting but impossible to locate. This kind of group activity (see section on 'Group behaviour'), although low-level in nature, can be extremely frustrating. It is not an understandable by-product of someone's anger or control issues – it is simply intended to cause annoyance. The more annoyed you become, the more amusing it will be to the culprits. If you choose to ignore it, however, it may not go away and it may, of course, get worse. Either way, there is no straightforward 'win'.

The crux of the problem is proof. The culprits will probably realize that if they remain sly and discreet, it will be hard for you to catch them out. If the behaviour is carefully coordinated, it may feel as if the whole class is against you. Even if you do have a strong sense of who is responsible, they will try to deny it and get their mates to back them up. Meanwhile, the pressure is on you to demonstrate to the class that you are in control; that a hardcore group of miscreants are NOT going to get the better of you. Sounds familiar?

This sort of behaviour is designed to test the boundaries, which suggests that students are looking for you to enforce them – so do so, but in a calm, matter-of-fact way. Don't try to outwit or bluff them into thinking you know exactly who's involved (unless you do), as this can quickly backfire. Simply be honest:

'Someone is making a humming sound. That person knows that I don't know who they are, but the problem is, it's not just me that's being affected by it. It's disturbing everyone, and it's wasting everyone's time. It needs to stop.'

Reinforce this message by focusing on the students who are being sensible – give them lots of attention, praise and reward. Other options include issuing a warning: unless the noise stops, the class will be kept in. However, this is very contentious. It *can* be effective, in that it uses peer pressure and establishes a clear consequence, but many would argue that it is unfair to punish the majority for the actions of a few. I'm inclined to agree.

Alternatively, diffusing the behaviour with humour can be an effective intervention, for example: 'If you're going to whistle, at least do it in tune!' or 'Can you sing instead – because your humming is lousy!' It allows you to maintain a positive atmosphere and shows that you are not easily ruffled. This tactic, however, is dependent on your teaching personality and your relationship with the class. One final suggestion is that you call in the old trust/respect issue. A firm discussion on the topic can have a powerful impact:

'I need to be able to trust you. If I can trust you then I will be happy doing fun activities with you and our lessons will be very enjoyable. How can you show me that you are trustworthy?'

USEFUL PHRASES

This section provides suggestions for how to talk to students. Sometimes the most effective words or phrases are not the ones we would automatically or instinctively use, but with practice they may become a more natural part of our classroom practice. The list is by no means exhaustive, but will provide some useful prompts:

1.   *Language of choice:*
         '*You need to* take your feet off the desk *or you will have to* move to the chair in front of me.'

'*When you have* completed two paragraphs of writing *then you can* go on the computer.'

2.   *'I' centred rather than 'you always':*
     '*I find it difficult to* talk to the class when you are chatting over the top of me, *so I need you to* stay quiet and listen.'

3.   *Criticism with praise:*
     'You are an important member of this class, *so* I don't want you to miss out on any opportunities because of your behaviour.'

4.   *Separating the behaviour from the student:*
     'I like having you in my lessons but I don't want to see that behaviour.'

5.   *Paraphrasing:*
     '*So what you are saying is* that you swore at David because he was calling you names?'
     '*From your point of view* Mr Jakes was being unfair because you didn't know you were supposed to be sitting down ...'

6.   *Positive phrasing:*
     'Sit up, face forward and show me you're ready to listen, thank you!' rather than 'Stop talking and lazing about!'

7.   *'Thank you' instead of 'please':*
     'I'd like to see you enter the room quietly, thank you.' which is more emphatic than 'Please will you come in quietly.'

VERBAL COMMUNICATION

Teaching is all about communication, so it is important that we value and develop our skills in this area. Some people find it comes naturally and are confident in front of the class from the start. Others learn through experience and practice, and may take a bit more time to feel comfortable in front of their audience. One of the key areas in which our communication skills become important is in dealing with challenging behaviour. This is where they can really be tested, because if we are confronted with a problem we have a number of things to think about:

- How can we make an impact and get students' attention?
- What can we say to diffuse the problem and avoid argument?
- What are the words/phrases that will make our expectations clear?
- How can we use our tone of voice to manage the situation?
- How can we stop ourselves from snapping/expressing anger?
- What can we say if we are not being listened to?

On top of this, we have to think on our feet and react quickly, but also think ahead. It helps if we can anticipate and plan for what might happen next. For ideas relating to the above questions see sections on 'Choice', 'De-escalation', 'Coping' and 'Useful phrases'. Effective verbal communication is something that can be learned. It may not be the kind of communication we are used to using in our personal lives – if someone tries to wind me up I'm more likely to express my true feelings, than calmly tell them they 'need to stop/think about the rule for respect/make the right choice'! We can think of it as a professional skill, another one to add to the job description.

VIOLENCE

The issue of fighting between students has been considered separately (see section on 'Fighting'), so this section will concentrate on the physical assault of members of staff. Having worked in schools for students with behavioural difficulties, I have received my fair share of pinches, kicks and threats, and over time, I have learned to deal with these calmly. However, I appreciate that the majority of teachers, at both primary and secondary level, do not come to work expecting to be attacked by their students, and such an experience may be very traumatic for them. Fortunately, statistics show that violent behaviour in the classroom is actually fairly rare, and is generally isolated to a few core individuals. Nevertheless, it can be frightening and stressful for those involved, and should always be treated very seriously.

Whether you have experienced violence against yourself or feel you are at risk (and this can include the threat of violence, as well as actual physical assault), it is important to have a plan of action that focuses on preventative measures, and provides some stability in the event of a crisis situation. In terms of prevention you will need to:

- Watch your own behaviour. Make sure you are not making the problem worse by reacting aggressively or threateningly, or making provocative comments.
- Identify your students' triggers. Be sure that you are aware and have an understanding of students' needs, whether they are related to work, emotion or behaviour.

- Familiarize yourself with the warning signs. If a student is getting worked up or angry, what does their behaviour commonly look like (e.g. furrowed brow, raised voice, restlessness, etc.)?
- Intervene early. Use low-level, calm interventions (such as redirecting a student to another area of the room, expressing empathy: 'I can see you are quite annoyed', giving calm, reassuring instructions, using choice) as soon as you sense a problem – things can spiral out of control very quickly.
- Use techniques to de-escalate (see section on 'De-escalation'). Remain calm, firm and polite, allow the student to have breathing space and avoid engaging in power struggles.
- Step back if necessary. Recognize that if you are the one that the student is wound up about (rightly or wrongly) it may be more prudent for you to step out of the situation and allow another member of staff to take over. This is not a sign of weakness.

If you are on the receiving end of an assault, you may initially experience shock. The chances are the rest of your class will be shocked too. This is a natural reaction to an unexpected and unpleasant event. You may also experience sudden anger, or the urge to retaliate. Again, this is a perfectly human reaction to the alarm of the situation, however, for your own protection, it is one that is best overcome. Your instinct may also tell you to just walk out of the room, which is understandable: you may be physically hurt, you may be upset and you may also feel humiliated. Why would you want to remain in front of the class, or, indeed, in front of the person who did this to you (if they haven't already run off)? In this instance, notify the nearest staff member. Hopefully, they will alert a senior member of staff, organize for your class to be looked after by another teacher and ensure that your physical and emotional injuries are tended to.

In the long term, you should expect that management allow you time to get your head together, whether this a cup of coffee in the staff room or the rest of the day off. You will need to fill out an incident report as soon after the event as possible. You should expect management to investigate and keep you informed of what action will be taken against the student who assaulted you. Such serious behaviour should result in some level of fixed-term exclusion, and at the very least, you should not have to work with the student again, until and unless your differences have been reconciled. It is absolutely unacceptable for any student who has assaulted a staff member to be sent back to class the following lesson without any agreement, apology or discussion – but unfortunately it happens. If you are not happy with the outcomes of the situation you may wish to contact your union, or even the police. If assault from a student occurs outside the school grounds it becomes a police matter automatically.

IS FOR...

WARNINGS

Warnings are an important part of any behaviour management programme. They act as a buffer between the problematic behaviour and the breakdown of cooperation. If cooperation is the thing we are all striving for, then it makes sense to do what we can to encourage and preserve it. By issuing a warning we are giving the student a chance to turn their behaviour around:

'You need to stop calling out whilst I'm talking to the class. This is your first warning. You need to stop or you will have to stay back after class.'

Not only does this discourage inappropriate behaviour, but it also encourages students to take control of their own actions and responsibilities. It forces them to manage their own choices. For the teacher, it allows a sliding scale of intervention that can get progressively more 'heavy' should the behaviour escalate, and therefore avoids the complication of running out of consequences.

For warnings to be effective, they need to be used to regularly and consistently, as their success relies on students realizing that there are definite consequences to not following them. I would say one or two warnings are enough. If a student fails to cooperate after that, then a sanction should be applied (see section on 'Consequences'). Be firm on this, even though it may take up a bit of your time and energy. Any more than two warnings, and the whole process can become a bit flabby. There is nothing less effective than a teacher who issues warning after warning but never follows up on anything. One particularly useful suggestion I have come across is making a written note of your student's behaviour. If things improve then you can show them that you are screwing up the paper and throwing it away. If they don't improve, then keep the note till the end of the lesson and take them to task on it, or explain that you will be showing it to their tutor/Head of Year/parents. It is a subtle way of giving a warning without having to waste your voice, or become overly distracted from teaching.

WELCOMING ENVIRONMENT

An often underestimated factor in student behaviour is whether or not a child/young person feels as though they are welcome in school. For students who have frequent difficulties, the experience of being in the school building can be largely negative. Even if they aren't doing anything wrong, it may well be expected of them – their reputation will precede them. Unfortunately, such assumptions, however realistic they are, can become a self-fulfilling prophecy:

'Everyone expects me to muck about. I'll probably get blamed anyway, so I might as well ...'

I believe that this plays a significant part in why some students find it so hard to change their ways. They become trapped in destructive patterns of behaviour, which are frequently reinforced by the expectations of the people around them. At the same time, their self-esteem is being battered by the negativity they themselves are perpetuating, making it harder to see the light at the end of the tunnel.

You will not be able to speak for the rest of the staff in your school, some of whom will have very strong (and perhaps dubious) opinions about what they would do with that little so-and-so if it were legal, but you can endeavour to make your own classroom a positive, welcoming environment for *all* students. If you are the teacher that is giving the problem student a break, the chances are, they will respond favourably to you. They may not be angelic, but if you show them that you are determined to help them succeed and have positive experiences, then you will be making an important connection with them – one that will help them to develop trusting, respectful relationships with adults.

DATE DUE

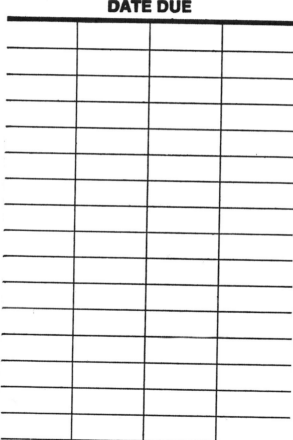